A PLACE IN THE WORLD

A Place in the World

IN THE WORLD

FINDING THE MEANING OF HOME

Frances Mayes

CROWN
NEW YORK

LIBRARY OF CONGRESS CATALOGING-IN-PUBLICATION DATA
NAMES: Mayes, Frances, author.
TITLE: A place in the world / Frances Mayes.
DESCRIPTION: First edition. | New York: Crown, [2022]
IDENTIFIERS: LCCN 2022016137 (print) | LCCN 2022016138 (ebook) |
ISBN 9780593443330 (hardcover; acid-free paper)
| ISBN 9780593443347 (ebook)
SUBJECTS: LCSH: Mayes, Frances—Travel. | Mayes, Frances—
Homes and haunts. | Women authors, American—20th century—
Biography. | LCGFT: Travel writing. | Essays.
CLASSIFICATION: LCC PS3563.A956 P57 2022 (print) |
LCC PS3563.A956 (ebook) | DDC 813/.54
[B]—dc23/eng/20220406
LC record available at https://lccn.loc.gov/2022016137
LC ebook record available at https://lccn.loc.gov/2022016138

Printed in Canada on acid-free paper

crownpublishing.com

2 4 6 8 9 7 5 3 1

FIRST EDITION

Book design by Barbara M. Bachman

FOR PETER GINSBERG,
VISIONARY AGENT AND FRIEND

AND IN MEMORY OF
AUDREY WELLS AND CHARLIE CONRAD

. . . how difficult it is to remain just one person,
for our house is open, there are no keys in the doors,
and invisible guests come in and out at will.

—*Czesław Miłosz, "Ars Poetica"*

Perhaps home is not a place but
an irrevocable condition.

—*James Baldwin, Giovanni's Room*

The house is the same size as the world,
or rather it is the world.

—*Jorge Luis Borges, "The House of Asterion"*

PREFACE:
I COULD LIVE HERE

THE SPRAWLING WHITE FARMHOUSE LOOMS IN MY HEAD-lights. I always seem to arrive home from my travels at night. Stepping out of the car, I'm hit by the fecund smell of the Eno River, which cuts through our meadow, wet grass (needs mowing), the greeny scent rising from a thousand trees, and the sound of screeching tree frogs. If it's early summer, any breeze wafts the divine sweetness of magnolia and tea olive. In winter, winking string lights along the porch cast light onto the bumpy stone path that ruins the wheels of my roll-on. In deep summer, bright sparks of fireflies, in autumn the crunch of fallen walnuts, and a clutch of purple asters around the back door. Kiss the ground. Pull the door to you or the key won't turn. Then it does. Anyone home?

Home: where and why *this* house? Is home fixed forever or a moveable concept? How do four walls, utilitarian and convenient, or soulful and evocative, connect with your me-tabolism and turn into that charged feeling of *I'm home?* Or is home a quest never to be fulfilled? Down the road not taken— was there a blue door for you to open? Some writer said, "My home is my subjects." What a floating idea of home. Mine feels more visceral. Most alluring, the places where you feel an immediate, illogical bonding. You wish you lived there but you never will. Capri, San Miguel, Provence—you imagine yourself extant in another version that may for years run parallel to the road taken. What's the truth—that hotel that caused me to refer to it as home after three days, or the house where I grew up? The first eighteen years: the spool bed, the mirror above the pink-skirted dressing table, ceiling fan pulling in a humid breeze over the buffer of hydrangeas around the house. Others? A boxy apartment at Stanford, where through thin walls I heard my neighbor cry out that Kennedy was shot. The New England saltbox in Bedford, prim black and white, where snow came up to the windowsills and lilacs surrounded three sides of the house. On Hamilton Avenue in Palo Alto, the L-shaped house, the inside of the L all glass. Orange, lemon, loquat trees. My Selectric typewriter on a picnic table by the pool, poems blowing into the water. My San Francisco Victorian flat where I became single after years of marriage? That first night, surrounded by packing boxes, the foghorns sounded like strange, mournful calls from far under the ocean.

I've always loved suitcases. The luggage rack stays up in my bedroom. That damp stone house above Florence, where bats flew around the fireplace. The *gullet* in Turkey where ten of us slept on cushions under stars, while the rigging clinked time with the swells. Home for a month, a whitewashed cottage in Crete, with bougainvillea blossoms wafting down the hallway. The rented house in Sicily can pull me back. I'm in the kitchen deciding what to cook and where I'll find a private spot to write about how we live there. Long after the key is returned, I'll revisit what Virginia Woolf called "moments of being." Is where you are who you are? Maybe home is as small as a suitcase.

I'm not looking for answers, but for more and more questions about what home means, how it hooks the past and pushes into the future. Often, it's mysterious. When my daughter was young, we lived in Somers, New York. In 1768, a man named Joseph Sunderland hid his account books—elaborately penned in black ink—along with seven thick sheepskin condoms in the rafters. Over two hundred years they waited for me—why me?—to reach behind a beam and bring them back. A millwright and maker of coffins. Enamored of a maid who lived in the attic room? We skated at night on Dean's Pond. Maybe he did, too. The old places we love will bring up the question that haunted medieval poetry: *Ubi sunt* . . . Where are . . . Short for *ubi sunt qui ante nos fuerunt,* where are those who went before us. Who left a coin between the floorboards, a date scratched on the chimney, the growth chart on the door? At Chatwood, my home in North Carolina, the name Buck was painted inside the barn door, and when I entered, I always sensed a black horse. These homes are vast and dazzling to the imagination.

This memoir is a floor plan of a lifetime of house and home obsession.

Maybe each chapter is a room in the big house.

Contents

VII: *Why Stay?*

INTRODUCTION:
IMPRINT

As a child in Fitzgerald, Georgia, way back in the middle of the last century (that sounds archaic), I was struck with the wildness of the land. I felt the elemental potency beneath my black patent Mary Janes (polished with Vaseline). Quicksand could take the dog. A tornado might rip every trailer and shack into the sky. Collapsing limestone layers could swallow a house whole—only a crooked chimney visible in the sudden chasm. Or the river floods, jumps its banks, sending a shack drifting, forlorn family riding the roof. The air rising above asphalt roads shimmied in the heat, oncoming cars quivering like mirages. Sheet lightning flashes like shook foil. There was, too, the acidic sweetness of roadside plums in the country, the dense scent of cotton fields after rain, lurid sunsets, water moccasins the size of my leg, icy springs bubbling out of the ground, and ten thousand other ways that I felt the innate energy of the place slapping me into a visceral identification with our plot of earth. Clear as the outlines of a saucer magnolia: the southern instinct for place.

Then came the home-bred writers, spoon-feeding me: Marjorie Kinnan Rawlings—I'll never get beyond *The Yearling*—and her beloved homestead, a cracker farmhouse deep in the orange groves of north Florida. At twelve, propped in bed, turning the pages of *Gone with the Wind*, what I was enchanted by was not the plot, the Civil War, or Scarlett and Rhett. I was hit by Tara, the iconic house. I absorbed the message: Home means more than anything. Later, I found Flannery O'Connor nailing her place to the ground, Thomas Wolfe in a boardinghouse in Asheville, elegiac and lyrical, Edgar Allan Poe, all dire and sad, Carson McCullers, who had the guts to begin a book "In the town there were two mutes, and they were always together." Zora Neale Hurston, digging back into witchcraft, spells, folklore, with her philosophy of being too busy sharpening her oyster knife to bother with what others thought she should be bothered with. Frank Yerby! The librarian disapproved of my voracious reading of his steamy novels that featured keys being passed to forbidden lovers and thrilling affairs. I read and reread Eudora Welty, that going-to-ground writer, living at home with her mother, her homespun magic and gigantic talent.

Then my soul mate: James Agee. His sense of beauty in every crevice, his tragic love of place, and his gift for taking you there. And over us all, looming at five feet four inches, cross yourself as you say his name: William Faulkner, epic father, lonesome homebody.

I already had the place inside, but when the writers came to me in high school and college, they named the nameless and thereby pinned me to their pages. Home. A place in the sun. Home, briar-caught, Christ-haunted, peopled by the living and the dead. Homebody me. The house: one's body living in another form. Homegrown. The idea burrowed into the canaliculi of my brain. Home place. To this day I can touch every inch of the house where I grew up—where the doodlebugs burrowed under the hydrangeas, my mother's yellow mixing bowls, unraveling ropes that raised the windows, climbing peavine on the front porch, the little iron door on the outside of the chimney where ashes fell out, my twin white spool beds with pink linen bedspreads scalloped along the edge, boxes of bullets and hunting rifles stored in the back of my closet. Such memories rise into a different consciousness of that time and might seem suspect viewed with a long lens, especially from those with set ideas of the South. No one is more aware of the ramifications of racial dynamics in the past than thoughtful southerners, of all races. To those who question any positive memory, I can only quote Federico García Lorca: "Beneath all the statistics / there is a drop of duck's blood."

Wherever I live, the house feels alive. Even in graduate school and newly married, a sudden startled homemaker, I began buying bargain antiques at auction, envisioning a romantic atelier in the university-provided apartment. I was imprinted with my mother's quest for the ideal house, with not a remote chance of living in one.

Then, grown and married, a saltbox in Massachusetts, a 1743 village house in New York, the low, L-shaped Palo Alto house with loquat and orange trees pressing close to so much glass. East coast, west coast—first for schools, then for work, for life. Moving went against my instinct for the taproot place one passes on to the next generation, but we moved. I resisted. Accommodated. And moved. For my husband's work. Through peregrine years of raising my daughter, living in a marriage—all exciting, tumultuous years—I wrote poetry.

And I painted and wallpapered and stripped and refinished. I cooked. This came from the love of it and living on graduate student scholarships, but also I still was answering some call from the Deep South sense of place that I inherited naturally.

Once settled, I loved New York, Boston, San Francisco, every place I lived, but what widened the aperture was where I traveled. London, Paris, Rome, Venice. I fell hard for Central America and Mexico. Unhooked from the South, in each country I now had fantasies that I could upend my life and live there forever. I wrote six books of poetry and a field guide, *The Discovery of Poetry*.

One July (fast-forwarding), after my marriage to my brilliant college boyfriend ended, I rented a house in Tuscany with friends. Rural life in those ancient hills simply knocked me in the head. After several more summers in sun-drenched villages, I forked over all my savings and bought a long-abandoned country villa. The life I forged caused a personal tectonic shift. The place had formed the inhabitants as surely as in creation tales where humans were patted into shape from mud. I was riveted by Italian time—long sine waves of artists, farms, history, piazzas, vineyards, cuisine—but, really, what I loved was the lively intersection of place with people. A vivid homecoming.

In Italy, learning a new language, soaking in piazza life, restoring a house, meeting people from all over the world, my poetry refused to break into lines; stanzas reverted to the actual meaning of the word: *stanza* = room. I bought a bigger notebook. My concept of time expanded and cubed. My fatalism subdued. I moved toward memoir as I felt myself begin to be changed by the place. The happiness that suffuses my Tuscan days drove my pen. I wanted, with my net, to catch elusive and fragile happiness in images. I was at home in Tuscany. Home free. As I thought more about the why of that, I embarked on a travel narrative originally called *At Home in the World*. When I found out another book already had that title, I changed it to *A Year in the World*. I explored what it would be like to live in other countries, some new to me and others that had attracted me on previous visits: France, England, Wales, Greece, Portugal, Spain, Morocco, Turkey. Traveling became not just travel but a choice of living a new way. I learned to see a place from the inside out rather than as a visitor passing through. Renting houses, apartments, even a boat, turned into a way of asking: What is home here? Who are these people and how has *here* caused them to be who they are? Home truths. I found out I could be at ease in the Arab quarter of Lisbon, in a former schoolhouse in the Cotswolds, in a whitewashed cottage in Crete with bougainvillea blossoms blowing down the hall from the open door.

Although my taproot led me to think of home as a fixed place, home became a portable emotion. Possibly this is genetic? Built into the DNA like a bird's instinct for migration. Or not. Carson McCullers writes:

It is a curious emotion, this certain homesickness I have in mind. With Americans, it is a national trait, as native to us as the rollercoaster or the jukebox. It is no simple longing for the hometown or country of our birth. The emotion is Janus-faced: we are torn between a nostalgia for the familiar and an urge for the foreign and strange. As often as not, we are homesick most for the places we have never known.

The poet Pablo Neruda claimed there are only eleven subjects to write about. He doesn't say what they are, but one of them, and the most difficult, must be happiness. Another must be home. Both subjects are hard to sustain; often they're entwined quests. Happiness: How to write a book that has no tense plot, an unforeseeable resolution, and not even an *I survived* motif? Well, I thought as I began writing about Italy, let's just go a little against the grain. I quit worrying about conflict/resolution and character development requirements. I'll try, I told myself, simply to re-create this place in tactile, evocative words. The writing felt spontaneous. When you're falling in love, everything is lit from within. When you're falling in love, you're greedy and generous, lavishing your insatiable desires over all you encounter.

At the end of writing *Every Day in Tuscany*, my third memoir, I decided to leave my home in San Francisco and return to my origins—the South. (My family always claims that I took the first thing smoking on the runway out of there, forgetting that there was no runway then. I'd had the instinct that, as a woman, I would forever be stalled by someone sidling up saying, "Buy the little lady a drink?" Or by well-meaning good ol' boys wanting an ornament by their side at the club.) My husband, Ed, was up for the move. He went to graduate school in Virginia and felt a strong connection to the gentle southern seasons. And the better proximity to Italy.

Back in North Carolina, we didn't locate the right place

right away. First, we lived in a columned house with a pretty view of a golf course. With some irony we called it Magnolia Hall. Out walking with a friend one morning, she showed me her friends' farm on the Eno River. She said she thought they were selling. Jokingly I said, "I'll buy it." A few months later she called. "They're moving to California." Ed and I walked around the grounds and fell under a spell. We bought the historic farm with extensive gardens in Hillsborough. I thought, now that I was getting older, I would have a world there, one I wouldn't have to leave if fate had hard surprises in store for me. (Home to roost.) The agent kept calling it our "forever home," making me feel like a rescue dog. Then, all at once, this farmhouse suddenly takes my love, my time, my hard work. I realized that I would passionately belong to it (instead of it belonging to me).

How to understand this frequent shedding of skin? *Re-home*, what a weird word. What is home? I have lived in eight states and Italy and countless temporary perches. On insomniac nights I walk through all sixteen houses. (Homework?) Each one, truly home. Each one a change marker. (Home place.) Where much of what happens in life happens. The one I walked out of. (Home wrecker.) The crux and crucible. Where you are manifest. (Homespun.) Home became a shapeshifter.

On these spring nights before the arrival of mosquitoes, I take my glass of wine out in the backyard and look up at the stars. Remember what Earth shows us: You are a traveler. Stare up for a while and you know. On our blue ball, we're rounding the bend toward, then away from light. Our progress has no names, no stations along the way, only seasonal markers on Earth—the blending of spring into summer, into autumn, winter. We're falling into longer days, shorter nights; we reverse. Astounding—we are unconscious of the vast trip we are on every instant of our lives.

Outside on a May night, take a glimpse into space long enough to see the shift of a constellation. Catch the flare of a star that fell eons ago, its arc of light just reaching your eyes. Your back against the damp grass, you're wheeling into the unknown. Paradoxically, traveler, you feel at home.

I

A HOUSE
DOWN SOUTH

Lighting Seven Fireplaces

2010. CHATWOOD CAPTURED ME BECAUSE I THOUGHT IF I lived here, I never would want to move again. Here's the musical crystal ball: Shake it and snow swirls. The place never will change. The sturdy farmhouse, anchored by four chimneys, stands on a gentle rise. Above the front porch, the windows are not symmetrical. I like that. The roof is ugly and we will replace it with metal. There is a hidden hive, and I put my hand on the kitchen wall and feel the boards hum. The Eno River runs by, and I love the murky, tannic smell of rivers. On the edge of the woods a fresh stream jets out of the ground, cold and holy, and a tumbled stone foundation remains of the old springhouse, where generations kept their food chilled. And so I settled in, convinced that I'd grabbed a star out of the sky.

As fires always roar, and rain pours, so do farmhouses ramble. The porch running the length of a room converts into a sunroom, a favored spot on winter mornings. A bathroom becomes a closet, and a new bath is added. The lean-to shed converts to a kitchen. The floor plan sprawls like tiles on a Scrabble board. Add, subtract, multiply, divide: The attic becomes a reading room, another attic makes a good study. The house groans but accommodates.

From my upstairs window, I see a brick-walled three-room rose garden, a nymph statue that looks lascivious, and, beyond, the pleasing meadow stretching to the river. I took down a view-blocking, half-dead tree and planted camellias. This spring, I have a large half-moon cleared for a wildflower garden. Already a plot is turned over and a bench placed for viewing the blooms. Anticipation is half of gardening's pleasures.

If an old house is a book to read—and it is—the upstairs study may be my favorite chapter in this house's long history. In the 1920s, the paneled room where I'm writing served as a fifteen-by-twenty-foot schoolhouse. An ancient neighbor recalled, "When the Altvaters moved in [1937], there were still at least a dozen school desks, homemade pine boards with the seat for the next desk attached to the front, and pigeonholes on the desktops for pencils, ink, and erasers. Set in rows, the back desks used chairs along the wall." I'm charmed that a Miss Sally Miller was the teacher. I can see Miss Miller in flower-sprigged navy dress and white collar, a dozen farm children wearing overalls and flour-sack pinafores. Their rough shoes and chapped cheeks. The teacher builds a fire, and the room overheats, sending out the smell of Octagon soap, chalk dust, gum erasers. They pledge allegiance to the droopy flag in the corner. They call out the multiplication table; they learn Wordsworth's poem about daffodils because this house floats on a wave of trumpeting yellow blooms in spring. On a shelf, tin buckets hold their lunches. Cold sweet potatoes, biscuits, and syrup.

I like to conjure the long-ago children enthralled or trapped here on a late May day, close to summer vacation. When I'm stuck on a description, blanking out for a next line, staring out the window, I'm cheered to think this was where they turned the thin pages of the Bible, saw a picture of Washington crossing the Delaware, and read Kipling's *The Jungle Book*. The first thing to know about living in an old house: The walls are alive.

This is not a dream study. I keep my desk, instead of a convenient one with drawers, because it reminds me of Virginia Woolf's. Sturdy columnar legs, worn patina of walnut, and a pocked leather top the color of old claret. Floor-to-ceiling bookshelves, others built under the windows, are jammed with my fiction collection, which I've never alphabetized. (Poetry and nonfiction are kept downstairs.) I can't find what I know I have. Despite four windows, the room is dark, and I hate gloomy rooms. I turn on the ceiling light, the two desk lamps, and the reading light beside a chair. Still not what you'd call bright, but the heart-pine walls send out a honeyed glow. On gloomy days, cozy, cozy. A fire feels cheery, especially when my two gentlemen cats choose my chairs for their naps.

The schoolroom is a relatively recent page in the saga of my house that creaks like a schooner (pegs and handmade nails working in and out) in the wind. I only can imagine most of the place's history. What I know comes from a few articles, a deceased neighbor's oral history, interviews, and a handful of letters in crabby handwriting that contradicts dates and sometimes veers into speculation. The earliest notes mention a Quaker named Isaac Lowe, one of a large family who held several land grants in Virginia. The land came to them in 1763 from the Earl of Chattharm or Chatthorn. I can't read the handwriting but am spooked that the first syllable of the name was repeated in the house's eventual name.

The first recorded house was built by other Quakers, the Faucettes, in the 1770s. When that burned, they rebuilt in 1806 or 1808 a plain but dignified Federal house of four large rooms, an attic room, and a kitchen. This is one of two of the period in North Carolina constructed for both commercial and residential space. We have two front doors because Robert Faucette, a miller, opened one into an inn and tavern, the other into his family residence. "Inn" sounds grand for the two rooms where sleepers must have piled onto corn-husk mattresses infested with mites, but each has a fireplace, mellow floors (some boards eighteen inches wide), and many-paned windows, which have bubbly glass that makes the view seem subterranean. When we remodeled the attic, we found Roman numerals carved into each succeeding beam and wooden pegs holding wall intersections together.

With frontage on the river and a quarter mile from a grist mill, traders and farmers brought their corn to be ground and had a place to stay if the water ran high. The Salisbury stagecoach came this way. General Cornwallis and his troops forded the river on February 26, 1781, en route to the Battle of Guilford Courthouse. Our narrow lane once was known as the Great Road, the Buffaloe Road, King's Highway, and before those as a native trading path for the Occaneechi tribe. As a coach forded the river, the driver sounded a bugle to let the innkeeper know it was arriving. Maybe Mrs. Faucette (no record of her given name) served roasted venison, wild turkey, and river catfish to hungry passengers.

The grist mill, operated into the 1920s, stands intact, though its wheel has been lost. There's a ghostly aura with a reason for that. Out walking, I always stop at a grave near the pond. Mallie Bryant, aged twelve, died in 1918. He fell out the mill's window onto cascading water and rocks. Elsewhere, a world war raged. Around his stone, daffodils pop up every spring. Under a hump of dirt next to him lies his mother, her grave unmarked because she died by suicide, unable to go on after her boy died.

During the 1930s, our house was brought back from ruin by the Altvater family. (*Altvater* means "high water," the situation that gave the earlier inn many customers.) Their daughter, Barrie, still owns the grist mill. She and her husband attached the home they built to a tiny mill keeper's house facing the river and pond.

Barrie's parents, Peggy and Vernon Altvater, added a wing onto the Coach House, as Chatwood was then called. At the southwest corner, Vernon attached another dwelling known as the Naile Johnson House, also a Federal period home rebuilt with pegs that he dismantled from its original location out on St. Mary's Road and from paneling and flooring from other old properties. The one very large room, and the upstairs over it, added space that the cramped Quaker innkeepers would have enjoyed. Can't you feel in your shoulders and spine when you've entered a well-proportioned room? Heart-pine floors gleam like dark amber. A great fireplace stands at the west end, flanked by windows with wavy glass panes that fill with sunset. The raised-panel mantel, the long-waxed paneled walls with bookcases and cabinets seem to have always been there. Most interior designers would walk in and slap pale Scandinavian wash over the walls. Although I felt the same impulse at first, now I never would paint away the warmth that seems to emanate from them. Few rooms I've entered in my life have personified *haven* to me, and this is one of them. Vernon Altvater couldn't know when he dismantled and hauled the Naile Johnson House how much pleasure he would give to someone eighty years later.

A gesture of his small son abides. On the door to the unfinished attic space that we transformed, I decipher the scrawling in crayon, barely legible: Wesley's Office KEEP OUT. Decades later, my grandson tacked his own PRIVATE notice in the same place. (How early the instinct for one's own sanctum occurs.) The low room, earlier, used to be the maid's quarters. A trapdoor opened to the kitchen below, and she climbed up by a ladder kept beside the fireplace. Since the early owners were Quakers, I hope "maid" in the records did not mean an enslaved woman. No way to know.

In the 1950s, the Coach House became Chatwood. The owners Charles and Helen Blake chose to honor the chat, a kind of thrush spotted on the property. Maybe they thought "Coach House" sounded like a kitschy restaurant. Helen Blake (later Watkins) began planting hundreds of bulbs, collecting local roses, laying out garden rooms with walls of Ligustrum, rugosa, barberry, boxwood, and holly hedges. I am tearing out some of those overgrown spaces. What vision. She hired a head gardener, two other full-time workers, as well as pruning experts, and rosarians for tending her grow-

ing collection filched from cemeteries, roadsides, and abandoned tenement and plantation sites. She energetically planted
specimen trees and dug up boxwoods. They thrive. When the
rare pale yellow magnolia blooms in early spring, I think of
her. She was hands-on, which remains a necessity. Does this
explain the source of my perpetual sense of anxiety over the
garden? How can I ever satisfy the insatiable needs?

Our current guesthouse served as a laboratory for Dr.
Charles Blake's ornithological studies. Retired from MIT, he
devoted his days to netting, identifying, and labeling birds.
He then sent them flying. He'd hear frequently from someone
in South America or Mexico who'd found a Chatwood-tagged
bird. The river and hardwood forest draw migrating flyovers.
Flocks pause, even murmurations, blackening the sky in their
mysterious patterns of swoops and reversals. Sometimes hundreds of crows home in. They shriek and caw, a visitation
from hell.

Reading on the sofa on a rainy afternoon, I could be in the
cabin of an old ship creaking with the roll of waves far at sea.
In the adjacent sunroom, Helen had her looms. What did she
weave? Did she undo at night what she wove that day? (Gardening can seem like that.) One photo of her survives, a
grayed-out Xerox from a newspaper. She has strong features,
upswept piles of hair that must have fallen to her waist when
she let it down. Or, wait, is that a bouffant wig? Surely not.
Sitting on a bench, she's solid as a tortoise. (Her bench still
stands—barely, with its arm about to fall off—under the
crape myrtles.)

What if we'd lived at the same time? What could I have
learned? She's just out of sight in the sunroom. In a slant of

spring light across her hands, she manipulates the heather-colored threads, warp and woof, soft slam of the loom, while I read *A Long, Long Way*, about an Irish boy caught in World War I. Mustard gas, the battle at Ypres. Helen's skeins of gold, coral, and sage. She who launched a thousand roses. Mallie's fatal free fall. And all the others whose lives flowed through here? Who married? Died? A pious Quaker wife with no name wringing the neck of a chicken. A boy listing his stamp collection in 1935, a yellowed slip of paper I find on the back shelf of a closet, undisturbed: Lincoln Douglas Debate, Noah Webster, Overland Mail . . . Helen's nimble fingers, pricked by thorns. My daughter crying over a lost love on New Year's Eve, and later a happy wedding by the fireplace in winter. My gray cat Hawthorn, killed by a neighbor's dog, sleeps in a shadow. No, that's a ball of heathery wool on the floor. The pink rose, Colette, brushes a window. White Sombreuil crawls along the chimney. The black snake coiled around the front doorknob. Who stokes the fire? Cuts the biscuits? We're reading and weaving the garden and filling the fireplaces in summer with shiny magnolia leaves. In winter, holly that pricks. Touch a bubble in the window glass with a forefinger. Glass is alive, moving. Scent of buttered toast, beeswax, soot, daphne. A nail works loose, slicing my foot. Vines pry into the sunroom, ivy, morning glory, kudzu creeping across the floor.

Who Lives Here?

If I may say so, what a nice town it is!

—BENJAMIN BRITTEN
(ON ALDEBURGH, SUFFOLK)

HILLSBOROUGH, CHATWOOD'S NEAREST TOWN, FEELS like the home I never left. When my family and I decided to move to North Carolina after decades in San Francisco, we kept hearing from friends in this area, "You must move to Hillsborough—that's where the writers and artists live." We were magnetized by the idea of a town where creativity might thrive, and having grown up in a small town in Georgia, I wanted to return to a place with an intense sense of community.

The decision was sealed when we first drove around the National Historic District. Everywhere on that late spring day, roses, jasmine, bluebells, irises, peonies, and wisteria bloomed profligately. Even on the 1768 map of Hillsborough, gardens are drawn next to houses, with notes such as "a formal parterre garden just to the east." It's easy to pull back the flimsy curtain of time and imagine tidy kitchen gardens, serpentine boxwood hedges, arbors heavy with muscadine grapes, somber cedar lanes, larkspur and hollyhock borders that reminded the early Scots, Irish, and English Quakers of their faraway homes. Many dignified early structures remain, some with intact covered wells and detached brick kitchens.

The district, more than four hundred acres of white houses and lofty trees, appeared to be a little Eden. Would time bear that out? Who lives here? Is this a place that encourages felicitous lives? Are there Klan members lurking in their garages, plotting something stupid? I spotted identical historic markers on houses with evocative names: Tamarind, Pilgrim's Rest, Twin Chimneys, Berry Brick House, Sans Souci, Sparrow, Seven Hearths, Heartsease, Elm Cottage, Burnside. When houses have names, they acquire an anthropomorphic presence, somehow causing the four walls to become more than the sum of parts. Houses named for their original inhabitants—Nash-Hooper, Webb, Newman, Scott—still hold on to their stories. Open the door and a host of lively people clamoring for attention fades into the hall behind the present owner. Even the mix of bungalows, cottages, and retro ranches among the older homes begins to look historic.

The houses are buoyed by circles of pink and white azaleas. I imagine a glimpse of summer: crape myrtles lining the sidewalks, breaking out into powdery mauve, milky rose, and white blossoms. In fall, so much autumn that you're thrown back to the earliest autumns of your life, when you first learned the smell of smoky leaves, roasting marshmallows, and the feel of running through raked golden and scarlet piles. Winter—well, winter is winter, but occasionally a layer of transforming snow will bring everyone out to revel in calm silence.

On that first visit, I followed the silver signs along Churton, the main street. Here's where the upstart Regulators acted up about taxes before the Revolution, where one William Hooper, signer of the Declaration of Independence, lived, where Billy Strayhorn, jazz composer and pianist, spent his childhood summers. At the historic Burwell School, a nineteenth-century girls' academy, the enslaved Elizabeth Keckley labored for the Burwell family. Eventually, through her talent as a seamstress, she bought her freedom and went on to sew for Mary Todd Lincoln.

I like wandering in cemeteries. What is more telling than how the dead are buried? In downtown Hillsborough's two graveyards, stacked stone walls among the plots speak of privacy and hierarchy. I would like to kneel among the obelisks and headstones with tracing paper and decipher some of the many epitaphs on the weathered tombstones. Those I can read are pious and hopeful, and occasionally personal. The last words a woman spoke to her children were "Be good and meet me in heaven." On another's, how grudging the "She hath done what she could," which smacks of an ungrateful family. If it had been Sunday, I could have visited all five antebellum churches. I slipped into the gently gothic St. Matthew's Episcopal Church, built in 1825, where I basked in the stained-glass light, and imagined scenes in English novels, where something that needed to be said was not. On the edge of the historic district, a park with enormous trees originally was a cemetery for enslaved people, the few known graves unmarked. A green enclave for contemplation.

Wandering outside the historic district, you quickly see that this town is chockablock with quirky residents who cherish—and flaunt—a highly individualistic sense of home. I spot many bottle trees, whose blue glass may or may not protect you from evil spirits, collections of artistic birdhouses, front porches, yes, furnished with the requisite rocking chairs but in hot pink. One keeps a derelict piano by the front door. Driving the side streets, I glimpse Celtic crosses, beehives, unpainted barns, plastic swans, and even one yard profuse with lurid fake flowers inside worn-out tires. The long-shuttered cotton mill, now renovated, gives this serial restorer fantasies of big-windowed lofts, and a cozy farm-to-table southern restaurant. The fate of such places is written; now the magicians must appear. Already, the mill neighborhood rises—a few shops, destinations for coffee, pizza, barbecue, and a down-home bar where people drop in after dinner for the live music. When we did, a bony woman maybe in her eighties asked me to dance.

WE BOUGHT OUR HOUSE made of dreams two miles out of town, where I fell into gardening and restoration. I spent mornings at the library learning about the history of Orange, as Hillsborough was originally called, and found in the locked glass case *Gardens of Old Hillsborough,* 1971, edited by Mrs. Charles H. Blake. Ah! A previous owner of my house and the author of its gardens. Writing back then about every rose in Hillsborough, she must have been sending a long cast forward hoping to catch the person who now tends her old musk roses decades after she is gone.

As soon as I unpacked, I set about reading the important books of the many writers in residence here. What a cache of brilliance. Does any small town anywhere have as many novelists, poets, and nonfiction writers within its borders? Soon we joined the throngs dining along Churton Street on Last Friday, a monthly get-together for all, with music on the courthouse lawn and the bookstore and galleries open late. We can't miss the strictly local parades. Who could not appear to see majorettes and dance schools, vintage trucks, and scouts tossing peppermints to the crowd? Taking up a new life in Hillsborough was easy. Why were we not here sooner?

By now, I've walked every street. Everyone walks. The dogs of choice? Labs. There are a few Westies, beagles, Jack Russells, mongrels, labradoodles, and cockapoos. But there are mostly gentle golden Labs. That kind of town. Chocolate shop. Home-grown art galleries. Bars with umbrellas and benches along the sidewalk. Sometimes a raised truck trolls by and a menacing Bubba malevolently looks out. He's flying the Stars and Bars, a throwback to benighted times. "Bless his heart," my friend Lee says acidly. I look away, remembering a line from *Deliverance:* "You have entered the land of the nine-fingered people." A favorite trek is the River Walk, paved paths meandering along the Eno. You stay near town but in the woods, listening to falling water, spotting the beautiful but poisonous jimsonweed flowers, sipping coffee picked up at Weaver Street Market, all without attracting any ticks. Turtles sun on rocks. They feel you looking at them and plop into the water. I'm partial to towns that have a river running through.

As I'm strolling around neighborhoods, music floats out of windows, and someone tunes her fiddle on the front porch while two friends wait to begin "I'll Fly Away." As I pass, they start up. A plaintive, high voice follows me down the block. At the Saturday morning farmers' market, music accompanies the selection of baby beets, ready-to-go pizza dough, and butterbeans. Across from the coffee shop and in a Brick Alley nook, pick-up music surprises me. A lone guy plays guitar on the courthouse lawn. All the arts are natural in Hillsborough. At a friend's dinner party, a guest may share her gift of several arias, or everyone chooses parts and reads a play while the hors d'oeuvres are devoured. At your plate, you may find a scroll tied with ribbon, a poem to read aloud with dessert.

I expected fun: Southerners know how to squeeze joy from every moment, and the friendliness of the South remains as legendary and true as some of the region's less attractive qualities. But, coming here from San Francisco, where social events were penciled into the agenda weeks ahead, I've been overjoyed at spontaneity. "Come over for chicken livers and Janis Joplin," I find in my email, and "Big pink cocktails on my porch at six."

I returned to the South after a long quarrel with the place. Racism, sexist zeitgeist, anti-intellectualism, self-satisfaction. Men who refer to "my bride" after forty years of marriage. Those still hover, but this town, intolerant of such stupidity, is aspirational.

I came home and experienced, as in Tuscany, and as in my Georgia childhood, the grand day-to-day human exchange that can be so rare to find. Strike up a friendship with the couple at the next table and exchange numbers, chat with the woman loading her car with groceries next to yours, wave as a car passes you on your walk. Hear yourself called "honey," "darlin'," "sister." Move in and neighbors bring soup, fruit, jam, flowers, cake. Get sick, you're inundated.

One building I always stop to admire is the 1845 court-house. Lucky the town that surrounds such a classic structure! Four solid Doric columns, mellow brick, and a Greek temple facade—the building could not be more important for those who live nearby. And here's the town's heartbeat: the clock in the cupola. It dates to the 1760s—possibly a gift from King George III. Residents since then have revered and protected it through upheavals and moves from earlier locales. Here on the town square, we mark our hours.

GREEN WORLD

Everything here seems to need us.

—RAINER MARIA RILKE

A S EVERY GARDENER KNOWS, THE ETYMOLOGICAL ROOT of the word *paradise* means "enclosed garden." Enclosed or not, a garden can give you a contact high that's as close to paradise as we can get. Ed differs. "Blissful and bothersome," he says. No matter how many anemones and cosmos sway in the breeze, how many wafts of ginger lilies and daphne and mock orange drift around the porch, how scrumptious the basket of tomatoes, fennel, peppers, and radishes—there is always a mitigating force. As you survey the beds, you can't stop noticing: Things could be better. Weeds, fallen branches, yellowing remains of bluebells and hyacinths after blooming is over. And why, why did anyone ever plant ten walnut trees at the entrance, where guests can be conked on the head by falling nuts? Walnut tree roots send out a poison into the soil, preventing anything you want to grow from having a chance. Why the perpetual glitch in the fountain (motor burned out again), the black spot on the Rosa Mundi, and the peach tree up and dying for no reason?

We have thirty acres here at Chatwood. Six—six—of those acres are cultivated gardens, including the glorious brick-walled rose garden inspired by one in Williamsburg, Virginia.

In the late 1950s, the owner and local legendary gardener Helen Blake's flowering rooms burgeoned, delineated by hedges and wide perennial borders. Her passion for roses flourished. She rustled whole bushes from abandoned farms and plantations, even taking slips from cemeteries before she became smitten with heritage French roses. By now, many have died, others have lost their tags, and often I'm not sure if a rose in question is the one marked as Prince Albert or Sir Thomas Lipton on her rose maps. Many twiggy remnants are roses unknown to modern catalogues and growers. Quickly, I realized that the research to pin down the names of the remaining roses could take half my life.

Moving here wasn't like buying a house with a few foundation plants, woody azaleas scattered about, and a front bed of annuals to be renewed in a day each spring. Chatwood, still a phenomenal garden, was a world-class garden seventy years ago. I've gone headfirst into several restorations, but this hits me over and over: I've inherited a phantom. This *paradiso*, eroded over the years, left me with plenty of garden maps to guide a stupendous restoration to glory. Sweeping over me next: I can't do it. So what will I do?

At its apogee, Helen tended more than 350 roses with few repeating varieties. Someone she obviously would look down on later planted the ubiquitous Peace in several spots. What a cliché, she clucks. I can see her, directing her head gardener and several minions to dig here, transplant there. Imperious, confident. Then I look down at my own ragged, dirty fingernails. Sixty-odd years after her reign, I consult her rose maps and struggle to replace ones that die. Antique roses usually bloom once and briefly, sending out fragrances I've smelled only in testing bottles at perfume counters. Her dead Ispahan I've replaced twice. I'm longing to see it thrive. See me at odd moments, scratching in the dirt for old tags, trying to read rusty ones remaining on twigs. When the bloom is on in late May, with rose books in hand—I am overwhelmed and enchanted. The names! I am stepping through the pages of Proust, through the Tuileries rose garden, around Josephine Bonaparte's Malmaison outside Paris, inhaling Colette's descriptions of her mother's Burgundian garden.

Read aloud her rose litany: Louise Odier, Cardinal de Richelieu, Fantin-Latour, Comte de Chambord, Aviateur Blériot, M. Tillier, Marie Pavié, Souvenir de La Malmaison, Cécile Brinmer, Mignonette, Louis Philippe, Mme. Pianzer, Clotilde Soupert (can't you just see Clotilde Soupert?), Amarette, Général Jacqueminot, Coquette Per Blanches (?—can't quite read her crabbed writing), Reines des Violettes, Duchesse de Montebello, Comtesse de Murinais, Charles de Mills, Duc de Guiche, Cramoisi des Alps, Henri Martin, Duc de FitzJames, Baronne Prévost, Mme. Zoetmans (isn't she peering at us through her lorgnette?), Alba Suaveolens, Cécile Brunmer, Souvenir d'Elise Vardon, Commandant Beaurepaire, Mme. Plantier, Albertine de la Grifferaie (I love Albertine), Mme. Les Gras de St. Germain, Gloire de France, Paul Perras, Sombreuil (a favorite), Hippolyte. Listing them feels heady. How I love the arduous rose garden.

The ghost of Helen Blake smirks. She's not so interested in the names. Fiddle-faddle. She's interested in why leaves roll up and drop off, why hundreds of iridescent beetles descend. Pick them off by hand and drop them in soapy water to die. What is that invasion of nutsedge? (One friend gave up gardening because of nutsedge.) It must be dug out way underground, where the evil proliferating nuts reside. She contemplates the oncoming challenge of spring. How to charm her roses into riotous bloom? Rotted manure. Epsom salts. Greensand. Alfalfa meal. Cottonseed meal. Fish emulsion. So many mocktails these roses imbibe. There's the rub—a real gardener marches into the garden as into battle. Instead, I feel like a neglectful mother who's allowed her child to run into the street. But then arrives the brief month of glory. This hallelujah season calls for a standing ovation. What's hard, Helen Blake: How to ignore the rest of the year when your rose garden looks quite bleak. I'm underplanting with dianthus and creeping thyme. Still, bare roses aren't lovely and you can just shut your mouth.

AS MUCH AS YOU own an old house and garden, it owns you. There's a continuum in progress. You've stepped in and now you're entranced and sweetly obligated to sow seeds in the vintage greenhouse, to plant the lettuces in ten-day intervals, to eat squash that keeps on coming long after you've had enough. At the same time, I want to shake it up. I simplify—reducing the size of several vast perennial beds with little remaining in them, staking vines, eliminating scraggly beds altogether, planting ground cover because the cost of weeding could send someone to college. We're organic. It costs more when you don't soak the ground with Roundup and

Sevin. Sorry, the homemade remedies just don't cut it on this scale. I would like to remove a row of awful and ancient cedars, all half dead inside, but the estimate was more than the price of a quite nice new car. I don't like mulch. It looks like corporate landscaping. The reddish kind looks like dog food.

Maybe even Helen would have cut back by now.

I've turned a two-room outbuilding full of dead crickets and fossilized fertilizer into an art studio and a writing retreat, living out a childhood desire for a playhouse. I had a scraggly Burford holly hedge ripped out, opening the view to long yellow flower beds. Ed and jack-of-all-trades Mr. Farley tied chains to the holly trunks, which looked like elephant legs, hooked them to a truck, and they came flying out of the ground. I almost expected screaming.

We added an oval swimming pool right in front of the weathered 1770 barn, which I hope to convert to a party room. I built a structure I call the Chapel of Hog Wire in the meadow and also a wire billboard, both for hanging art for an annual show, most recently celebrating the work of the brilliant landscape artist John Beerman. While wandering around the garden, a couple of hundred people sip wine, munch on sage-orange shortbread and tea sandwiches of pimiento cheese or watercress. The chapel is covered with climbing gourds and morning glories in full summer, a secret spot to read. My two cats think it's their house to climb. Everyone raves over the garden. I have brought it back to glory, I have kept the spirit, I have saved a piece of the patrimony. But the stream is getting blocked by weeds. The dahlias came up in garish red, not the pink I planted. The graceful crabapple tree appears to be succumbing to rot.

The truth dawns: I am giving over my life to Chatwood.

In the vegetable garden, surrounded by a picket fence to deter deer, we grow strawberries, cucumbers, clumps of zinnias, Rattlesnake watermelons, peppers, cardoon, herbs, squash—an overwhelming bounty to share. Okra, with its creamy hibiscus-like blooms, deserves a place in a flower bed. I have to feel sunny and carefree opening the gate with an empty basket on my arm, then leaving laden with gorgeous tomatoes, handfuls of herbs, and a bunch of zucchini flowers. One night when we were away, a doe leapt the 4.5-foot fence and inconveniently gave birth in the zinnia bed. She wouldn't leave her new one. Frantic, she destroyed everything. When the gardener came to mow and heard the thrashing, the doe was found and released with the tiny fawn. We're trying again. The soil is turned and raked, the greenhouse full of sprouted seeds. I've heard that leaving on a radio tuned to right-wing political talk shows scares away all creatures.

You can tell—I'm a dilettante gardener. "But wait," my husband insists, "you're a writer. You can't devote your life to bringing back a vast garden." But I love the hot peppers, the Dr. Van Fleet climbing over the garage, and elephant ears along the stream! Not prone to guilt, still, I can envision this little kingdom gone wild, coyotes encroaching, ivy twining around my ankle. I sense the rushes of that dark force my neglect might unleash. Therefore, I'm out early, face smeared with SPF 85 sunblock. Work in this heat, you melt like wax.

I OFTEN WALK DOWN to the edge of the woods to Springhouse Creek, with its remains of a springhouse. My two cats prance on the remaining stones and lap from the cold water that bubbles up. Ah, the original source for the house, still flowing pure and clean. The first daffodils—Chatwood has hundreds—come up around the half-fallen foundation in late January, and the first copperhead (trouble in paradise) rears its cunning head from a hole soon thereafter. I like to imagine Mrs. Faucette, wife of the Quaker who built Chatwood in 1806, bringing her ham, butter, and cheese to the shelves that once existed over the icy water that trickles up from underground. The stream flows from here into the Eno River. Will we ever clear the weeds and wade in the cold water all the way to the river? I can imagine the pleasure so intently that I think it has happened.

With our landscaping crew, we have hacked jungle brush and weed trees along the Eno, which inexplicably had been ignored as part of the garden. We hired men with major equipment to cut and dig and saw for two weeks. Suddenly the meadow extended to the water, a sweep of view across buttercup fields to the sparkling river my grandson says is the color of Coca-Cola. Ed bought an extension tool that clips high branches, and a new weed whacker. Months of work ensued. I knew we were in the garden's thrall when romantic Ed gave me a chain saw for Valentine's Day. We installed a culvert over another stream and now have access to a mile-long riverside walk. Our few neighbors walk on our land and we on theirs. The woods are full of laurel. The small pink blossoms remind me of a dotted-swiss sundress I wore when I was eight. An ineffable joy to walk along the Eno, to startle turtles who flop off logs, to see trees reflected on the glittering surface, and to find wild ginger and shy ferns peeking around rocks.

FROM THE FOLDER OF yellowed garden maps, I learned Chatwood's lost garden names—Horseshoe Garden, which I call Birdhouse Garden; Lake Bed, which is known now as Long Meadow; Secret Garden, now a circular stone terrace called Moon Terrace; Azalea Hill, now no azalea in sight, but what a good idea; Sundial Meadow (sundial MIA); and Maple Gate, known to me as Lower Gate. Always discoveries. We have added Brief Creek and Walnut Oval and Springhouse Creek and Wedding Parterre because we always hope someone will get married on the long terrace that steps down to the meadow. We live among many happy places where we imagine events that probably never will happen.

From Helen, and the owners after her, I inherited a fortune. I know to expect a pink knot of hyacinths to erupt by late February, an onslaught of daffodils and narcissus into March, pink columbine, bleeding heart; the wide swath of Virginia bluebells to pop out in April; and for May, the roses, clematis, and long border of fluffy Sarah Bernhardt peonies. (Beautiful as they are, I don't like the irises. Their sword-like leaves are ugly for much longer than the brief bloom.) Clumps of daylilies— they need separating—ginger lilies, calla lilies, and the true lilies Stargazer and Casa Blanca carry through midsummer, then phlox, echinacea, butterfly bushes, black-eyed Susans, and Japanese anemones save the day in high summer, when our southern gardens lapse into heat exhaustion.

Thank you all who came before me, enduring chiggers, ticks, poison ivy, sunburn, pulled muscles, stings. From my porch on a spring morning, I look out at the green world. Hello, I call out, just to hear the echo from beyond the trees. Hello, the air returns my voice. Or is it the land's voice? "There lives the dearest freshness deep down things," the poet Gerard Manley Hopkins wrote. A flash ago, winter blotted out color, leaving the garden palette monochromatic gray, dun, and black, with only boxwoods and cedars to spark the scene. Now I see jungle green through a scree of light rain, a rich terrarium with kaleidoscopic flowers running through their seasons of beauty, as we are whirling within the same cycles ourselves.

CAMELLIA

As MY FRIENDS ARRIVED, I HID UNDER MY BED. MY MOTHER searched the house and finally spotted a black patent Mary Jane protruding beyond the dust ruffle. "Come out of there this minute," she commanded. She dragged me to the party. Presents were stacked on the dining room table and my friends were drinking cups of punch. On a silver stand in the center of the table sat the cake my mother had made. Three layers tall with four candles, shiny white frosting, and rosettes of pale green, the cake was surrounded by soft pink flowers with shiny leaves. Camellias. And since, any pink camellia takes me that far back.

WHEN I BOUGHT CHATWOOD, I discovered that eighty-year-old camellias ruled the backyard, a dozen twenty-five-feet-tall mother bushes, each the circumference of a car. One produces solid blossoms next to others striped like ribbon candy. Who can get far enough back into the bush to see if there are two trunks? What luck—all these camellias are shades of pink, from faint blush to watermelon, their luminosity striking in the winter dusk.

I learned from inherited garden notebooks that when Hurricane Fran hit in 1996, this property lost seventeen giant trees, taking away much of the camellias' protective shade. They still bloom brilliantly but tarnish quickly, gracing the ground with a tapestry of fallen flowers. I contemplate pruning after the blooming season, but the interiors are dense. All summer, instead of flowers, I see the exits of birds, the ones who sing "bistro, bistro," and the ones who answer "T-shirt, T-shirt."

In the primeval South, I imagine sun-pierced woods dense with longleaf pines, laurel slicks, towering magnolias, and a proliferation of camellias among giant ferns. Not so. Although camellias are so deeply identified with southern gardens as to seem indigenous, they're latecomers (1700s), and of Asian origin. Could this be true? One called Pine Cone Scale, planted in 1347 during the Ming dynasty, survives in Yunnan Province at the temple of Panlong Monastery. This casts my near centenarians as infants.

The clue I should have picked up comes from the names of the three main types of camellia: japonica (from Japan), sazanka (a Japanese word for the smaller-flowered variety), and sinensis (camellia from China). All belong to the Theaceae family, meaning tea, and the sinensis with its small white flowers is where teas come from. I will pay attention when my camellias are blooming to see if I can detect a whiff of tea scent. Of the japonicas and sasanquas, there are more than three thousand named varieties—some resemble dahlias, carnations, roses, even gardenias. What choices!

I once visited Eudora Welty's restored garden in Jackson,

Mississippi. She and her mother, Chestina, loved camellias. Eudora studied in New York and her mother used to send up boxes of blooms on the train. (Imagine such train service!) After Columbia University, Eudora returned to live in Jackson, and she began to send favorite specimens to friends. "I sewed the stems to the inside edges of the boxes so they wouldn't move about or jostle and hit each other . . . I only tried to send four or five blooms in a box on overnight express and they'd get to New York the next day." Many plants in the Welty garden were selected by Chestina, but in a 1943 letter to the man she was in love with, Eudora wrote of planting a curve of seven camellias: Herme, Duc d'Orleans, Tri-Color, Elisabeth, Herme (again), Pink Perfection, and Leila (aka Catherine Cathcart), interspersing between them daffodils and a scattering of hyacinths, star flowers, irises, and tulips— a quintessential early spring mix. In homage, I planted several of her choices. I especially dote on Pink Perfection, not a great name but chillingly beautiful in its purity of form and color.

Among ten new bushes in a sheltered bed across the lawn, I chose Eleanor Hagood and Debutante, too, because they reminded me of the camellias I played under as a child. My hairstylist gave me a sack of blond, gray, and brown clippings, and I stuffed net bags to drape from the branches. Human hair is known to be a sure deer deterrent, since none of the men in the family seems interested in urinating on the plants. I scattered garlic. Within a couple of weeks, the leaves were stripped, stems gnawed to the pith. They survive as stragglers, lopsided and bloomless. Next time, wire cages.

———

SOME LONG-GONE OWNER PLANTED a jarring red camellia in front of a brick chimney. I thought of moving it—I prefer soft colors and don't like red in the garden—but soon realized that the color in drear January complements the cardinals that love to dart among the lustrous leaves and in the snow. This interloper has become a favorite. From our library's windows on either side of the fireplace, the vibrant blossoms press rosy faces against the glass and fill the winter view. The fire illuminates the intimate book-lined room. Hello, hello. Winter afternoon in this small world. Time to pour the tea.

MAGNOLIA

"WELL, HOW ARE YOU, MAGNOLIA, LOOKING PRETTY as ever," my brother-in-law always greeted a woman whose name he could not remember. (Men were designated "Coach.") Magnolia, of course, speaks metaphoric volumes: It heralds the woman as a flower, as mysterious and beautiful; it acknowledges her fragrant allure. And that flower of the South knew full well that Bill had no idea what her name was.

Magnolia grandiflora, a true native. Does any other flower have quite the mystique? The California poppy, Washington cherry, the Texas bluebonnet? Not a chance. They lack a perfume as strong as knockout drops, lack the magnitude of the creamy tight buds that open into face-size blossoms of extravagant beauty, and they lack gravitas. At the first funeral I ever attended, a full-open magnolia blossom lay on top of the gleaming, dark wood coffin. One was enough.

When I lived for many years in California, the lost scents of home haunted me most. Anytime I returned, I'd find myself outside after dinner, listening to the screeching chorus of tree frogs and night birds and just breathing in the layers of sweet, dank air. To me, moonlight smells like honeysuckle, or vice versa. When I was small, my bicycle leaned behind a bushy gardenia against the red barn. Cycling reminds me of the cloying, decadent presence of those flowers that bruised brown when I touched the petals.

I have all these scents and others in my North Carolina garden. I'm amazed when my scraggly daphne bush sends out heavenly blasts that no conjurer of scents ever came close to capturing in a bottle. Jasmine spreading around the front steps may be home for copperheads, but the narcotizing perfume rising to the porch compensates for that inconvenience.

When I moved in, I acquired an immense flowering garden with fragrances throughout summer: jasmine, honeysuckle, gardenia, rose—all the sweet whiffs on the breeze. Daphne surprises the winter air with its intoxicating breath of the tropics. In spring, kneel down in the grass to get close to the violets, muted and nostalgic. These are our magical scents, yes, but the truest *eau du South* remains the magnolia.

The big tree is as primitive as anything in a rain forest: leaves with undersides like suede riding chaps, tough cones, low limbs grabbing the ground and sprouting, dense vicious roots that crowd out anything trying to grow.

We have two towering magnolias, one far enough away from the house that the shed piles of tough leaves don't bother me, the other too close to my bedroom window. What goof plants a magnolia near the house? Though it blocks light, I love the sunlight glossing the leaves, especially when they're dusted with snow. And on a summer night when I raise the window, the soft, waxy sweetness of the ethereal flowers suffuses the room. That's when I think, "Why live anywhere else, ever?"

GARDENIA

A HUMID NIGHT WITH THE CAR WINDOWS DOWN, WE'RE parked, Max and I, on a side street in the Garden District of New Orleans. (*Parked* used to be a loaded word.) His mouth is like Michelangelo's *David*'s, and what an expert he is at using it. Hands, too, they look like they could shape and sculpt—me, perhaps. He loves poetry and the Russian novels I've recently devoured. I'm dazzled when he quotes the James Joyce "yes, I will" soliloquy, as I'm the romantic who imagines love as intertwined with quotes from Yeats and Keats, notes tied like scrolls, dancing on a terrace over the sea, reading under the willow tree, hearing someone say, "Twice or thrice have I loved thee before I knew your face or name." But wait, the sudden attraction to Max is his body, the muscular shoulders, blue shadow of stubble, a man, not the skinny boys I know. I've had sweaty make-out sessions on other hot summer nights. Not like this. He's engaged. But she's out of town and we've fallen in love and lust, equal measures. I'm visiting my college roommate for two weeks and Max is her brother. She disapproves of this surprising flare. The fiancée is a friend of hers. He's five years older, twenty-four. He looks like a young Hemingway. I'm wearing a scoop-necked white eyelet dress with a sash of burgundy, magenta, and rose velvet. I designed it myself. If I don't watch out, the delicate fabric will rip and what will I say to his mother, who waits up no matter how late we trail in? Rain suddenly pelts the fogged windshield and with it rises the heavy scent of gardenias. I turn from his arms to the open window. There, all the pale flowers, nodding and wan in moonlight. "Don't touch," my mother always warned when she brought in pristine blossoms to float in a crystal bowl, "or you'll spoil them."

I reach out, snap off a flower, and bring it close to his face. "You," I say. "You," he repeats. Such long kisses, breathing in each other, the cool erotic scent of gardenia imprinting, and words spoken, deep words I still heard the next morning when I boarded the train for Atlanta and never saw Max again.

After I met Ed, he asked, "What's your favorite flower?"

"The gardenia."

"Then I will have one beside your bed every day for the rest of your life." (That's romance.) After we moved in together, he was able to sustain the promise for about two weeks.

Years later, I told him about the steamy New Orleans night, the car suffused with the dense perfume of the wet gardenias. The night I had thought, *Keats can wait.* And I said that Max had married the traveling girlfriend.

I expected a flash of jealousy, at least. "Your mother," he responded. "The story is about your mother. The don't-touch-the-petals. Isn't it obvious? That's why you got on that train and went home."

He brings me roses. Always roses.

Sun Standing Still

—⚷—

OVERWHELMING. THAT WORD KEEPS BREAKING through the surface of my mind from mid-November until January. I make lists. I make lists of lists. For all my adult life, I've associated Thanksgiving with convivial fun and with exhaustion. Oh, yes, I love setting the big table and the adjacent tables with vintage monogrammed napkins, just-polished silver, writing the place cards, arranging the flowers, and even cooking for three days prior. I love my aunt Mary's corn bread stuffing, my mother's brown sugar muffins and cream gravy.

The actual dinner? It falls short of my expectations. Something's cold. I get stuck with a guest's guest who recounts endless medical appointments—the organ recital—and childhood anecdotes. The feast is over way too soon, leaving counters strewn with wineglasses and sad side dishes no one touched. All that work—and we're done?

Pulling out spiraling yards of foil, I give away all the leftovers. What remains of the twenty-five-pound turkey dries out quickly. If only I'd be allowed to prepare just the breast in the Italian way, opened and stuffed with pistachios, breadcrumbs, and veal, then tied, rolled, and roasted. That is not the way we do it at Thanksgiving. As ordained in the stars, the big bird is whole and basted and stuffed, and my husband will again review the carving video on his computer and perform handsomely at the table.

Before my daughter's childhood cutouts of turkeys and pilgrims are put away, before the tablecloths are ironed and stored, the next holiday rolls forward like a sneaker wave. Deck the halls! Every year, we all swear we will give one gift to each person—forget drawing names for only one gift, we're not that delusional. But we will simplify; we will not participate in the orgy of shopping, ordering, wrapping, delivering, consuming. We will make this holiday about food and friendship and warm evenings around the fire. We do that, yes, we do. We have lovely dinners for friends, we make our own wreaths. (Is that really worth it?) We bake and pack cheese straws, roasted pecans, and my mother's Martha Washington jetties in darling little boxes and distribute them among friends. But we succumb to amnesia and enter the fray like maniacs, fretting about what X would really like and is what we have for Y enough and what on earth can you give to Z, who has everything and then some? Suddenly, the tree is surrounded, knee-deep in gifts. I have the embarrassing memory of myself at nine or ten opening dozens of presents and at the end looking up innocently and asking, "Is that all?"

What to do? Give to charities, yes. Find a school with a program that makes sure children have pajamas, yes. Contribute to book programs. Adopt a star on the church's tree, ensuring holiday dinners for the community's needy. All that. Still, the holidays incite madness.

Why this end-of-year craze, when ". . . winter nights en-large / The number of their houres," as Thomas Campion wrote. I say there's something primordial at work.

Aside from the table laden with favorite morsels, and beneath the ribbons and wrapping paper and tissue and tape, something else mysterious is transpiring. Emotions turn fragile. Something in the rudimentary medulla recognizes the magnetic pull toward the darkest, longest night: the solstice, when the ancients thought the sun, in battle with darkness, might die, and therefore the earth, too. Solstice: sun standing still. If it went lower in the sky, it would disappear. Could it happen? Empirically, we think not, if we think about it at all, but instinct turning in the bone marrow sends forth doubt. In the oldest spirals of our DNA, we feel a vulnerability. We are here for a brief ride on this planet from which we soon will be flung again into the unknown we emerged from. Therefore, no matter what religion or pagan tradition your own solstice holidays might represent, what we most want to give our loved ones, we cannot. Giver and receiver know this without knowing it.

Hence the eternal *is that all?* Hence, the eternal *I'm not sure she really likes it.* Hence the private weeping in the bathroom and even the bourbon-fueled cousins fighting in the kitchen. The tears that well up in the department store when "O, Holy Night" loops around again.

The jolly end-of-the-year holidays are profound. On the shortest day, Earth swings toward light, and at that crux we feel the pith of life, the truth brought close. You throw out a silent message to the universe: Let us be. Let me have my home. The life I am living.

——

THE CRISIS PASSES. A little more light accrues each day. Wasn't it a lovely holiday after all? The white cat cavorts along the river path. Red camellias press against the frosted window glass. The soufflé hits the top of the oven; the boy loved the books. "Read to me," he says. Yes, I will. The biking windbreaker—exactly what the no-longer-rabid cousin dreamed of. He smiles. "Perfect for spring." "Amazing," my daughter exclaims as she pages through her new Israeli cookbook. "Let's go vegetarian." Everyone's cool.

"I'm glad it's over," my neighbor admits.

"Let's get that tree down before New Year's," my husband suggests.

I look up from my notebook where I'm listing projects, spring seeds to order, recipes. "Down so soon?" I say. "Not yet. Didn't I tell you? We're having fifty over on New Year's Day."

. . .

Martha Washington Jetties

Did Martha really make these delectable, chocolate-dipped, nutty fondant candies? I've prepared them every Christmas of my life, as did my mother, and now my daughter. Mother performed the chocolate bath on our cold back porch so the dip would set immediately. Fun to make, jetties will elicit major joy from those lucky enough to be given this gift. One seems like enough, since they are so rich; yet by the end of the day, the tray sits empty.

- First make fondant balls, about four dozen:

  ½ cup softened unsalted butter
  4 tablespoons heavy cream
  1 teaspoon vanilla extract
  1 pound confectioner's sugar, sifted
  1 cup chopped pecans

- Mix well the first three ingredients, then slowly work in the powdered sugar. Add pecans last. Roll the fondant into bite-size balls.
- Place them on two baking sheets lined with waxed paper.
- Chill well in the fridge.

CHOCOLATE DIP

  8 ounces semisweet, good-quality chocolate
  4 tablespoons unsalted butter
  5–6 drops vanilla extract
  3 tablespoons cream

- Melt together the chocolate and butter on very low heat in a small saucepan. Add vanilla and cream.
- Raise to simmer, then remove the pan to where you will work.
- Using toothpicks, quickly dip and swirl each ball in

the chocolate, coating the fondant all around. Place onto the waxed paper. If the chocolate starts to harden in the pan, briefly return it to the heat.

- When you've dipped all the balls, cover the little toothpick holes with chocolate to seal them.
- Chill again until well set. Peel the candies off the paper and place in gift tins. Keep in a cool place.

Secret Spaces

L OOKING FOR A HOUSE, YOU'RE GODLIKE. YOU'RE determining where the future will happen. You'll be the namer, marker of boundaries, creator. But you can feel similar to a fox gnawing its own trapped foot. Get me out of here. I just want to go home. House hunting is a fraught activity—and a strange one, too, because you may be set on counter space, walk-in closets, and a particular school district, but in the turmoil of the moment you fall prey to irrational forces from the deep past. Aunt Hazel's Spanish tile extravaganza, Aunt Mary's four-square farm in Vidalia. Fantasies arise from a remark overheard in line at the grocery store. "I just love her coral-and-sage great room." Suddenly you want a coral-and-sage great room, too.

Before I found Chatwood, when looking for the right home in North Carolina, I was shown a venerable white house with black shutters. I walked through, immediately crossing it off because of poky rooms and a narrow kitchen of gray Formica and linoleum. The agent spoke of remodeling, but I could see that load-bearing walls would have to go, meaning at least ten months of my life would also have to go before I could toss a salad. Besides, the café curtains, tiles printed with sprigs of herbs, and the Mixmaster were such period pieces that the Smithsonian should have transported the whole intact ensemble to Washington.

Then—here's the irrational. I walked out on the sagging back porch into a romantic English-style perennial and rose garden. All well and good; I can create that anywhere. But at the end of a lavender-bordered path stood a playhouse. A playhouse with a front porch covered with purple morning glories.

When I was little, I longed for this playhouse. My parents promised then forgot, then said no but allowed me a dim storage room in the barn behind our house. I arranged suitcases and camp trunks into beds and tables as best I could, filched spoons, baking pans, a glass swan, and a needlepoint cushion for my dog.

Here, decades later—what I once envisioned. Inside, I imagined the round table, just to scale, which I would set with miniature tin dishes and the opaline green tea set that my sister, off at college, didn't know I took from her closet. Under the window I would place the spool bed for dolls.

What remained was a shelf of books gone moldy and a teddy bear eviscerated by squirrels.

"You okay in there?" the agent called. She was making calls under a crape myrtle tree.

I was stunned silent. Backing out, I almost glimpsed a smaller me sipping sour-grass tea with my Alice doll in her finery and the baby dolls ranged around me, the inventor of their lives.

"You can't go home again," Thomas Wolfe asserted. What made him think that? Of course you can. Just don't expect anyone to answer the door. You can enter, you always can walk the rooms where you lived, where you were the you before you became you. Always, in three o'clock insomnia nights, you can hear (but not see) them back in the kitchen laughing, banging pots, pouring bourbon, squabbling over the last slice of pecan pie.

We did not buy that house. Ed was alarmed that a play-house, good lord, exerted such a pull that I might downplay a treacherous narrow staircase and bathrooms installed in the 1950s.

I snapped out of it and continued the rounds with the en-thusiastic agent. I'm enthralled with old houses. Having lived much of my adult life in Italy, I've learned how to bring the past along, rather than destroy and rebuild. Although I know the appeal of a tabula rasa new house, old ones surprise and intrigue me more. I've fallen for several. When the agent turned in at the lane leading to an upright farmhouse with book-end chimneys, a porch along the front, magnolia trees, and a meadow along a river, I was ready to sign the dotted line before I opened the car door. Ed agreed, this was Eden.

Inside, the house smelled like closed-up chapels I've come across in the Italian countryside. The kitchen fireplace had a swinging arm for hanging a pot over the coals. Copper sinks, bookcases everywhere, staircases that twist, many-paned windows splashed with green views—we are home. That fast. Many of life's momentous decisions come from such wholehearted and immediate responses. Even if the negatives of the decision arrive later, and arrive they do, one tends to have no regrets.

Like most farms, this one has outbuildings. We suddenly

owned a barn, toolshed, vintage greenhouse, three well houses, two rose-tending houses, and a rectangular white building about twelve by thirty feet of no known use. Two doors opened into small rooms packed with a chaos of solidified fertilizers, tangled hoses, rolls of wire, pots (some good), rusted watering cans, and thousands of crickets all leaping randomly on piles of detritus. A quick image of the playhouse flashed through my mind.

OVER TWO YEARS OF settling in, and, yes, dealing with the surprises (What? Kerosene radiators? What even *are* those?), I forgot the Cricket House, as we called it. Now and then I'd open the doors, stare a minute, and go away. One winter afternoon I was reading the local historical society's architecture monographs. I was drawn to descriptions of brick summer kitchens, several one-room law offices, a tiny schoolhouse, garden rooms, privies, and carriage houses. Driving around looking at them, I wondered why I wanted that playhouse when I was a child. Was it, as I first assumed, a desire to mimic on my scale the house of my family? To be a wife-in-training, honing domestic skills early? When I reinhabit that nine-year-old, I sense that the playhouse was more—a secret place of my own making. Yes, Virginia, that room of one's own. Suddenly, the clarity: Cricket House! Standing there. Two rooms waiting for transformation.

WITH THE GOOD HELP of a handyman, I haul and scrub and brush out insect carcasses and papery snakeskins. He cuts two windows, removes panels in the doors, and installs glass. Light! He tacks up insulation and covers the walls with ply-wood. Luckily, we have electricity. After a drastic cleaning of the concrete floors, we paint them a soft aqua, and the walls three coats of mascarpone white.

I do have a study in the house, but it's never been off-limits to anyone looking for keys, glasses, advice about a plane res-ervation, or asking what's for dinner. My grandson uploads, downloads, researches, plays with my computer. He, Ed, and I plan all our travels together there. My desk is dominated by a large computer—no space left for impractical tangents, books to spread out, drafts to compare. But now—two little rooms, empty, shining, waiting.

One for writing and reading. At a consignment store, I find a whitewashed wooden desk. I take metro shelving from the attic and buy a vintage wicker chair. All's spare and cool. The other space becomes an art studio with a door on saw-horses, an easel, a bulletin board posted with the art postcards I've gathered from museums. I am not an artist at all. The art room is fantasy. Here I cast around in architecture books, and paint swirly abstract watercolors no one will ever see. They are awful. I imagine that someday I'll paint something myste-rious in oils, something that will—ha!—unlock a hidden abil-ity I might have.

The doors face the back of an azalea bed. No one comes to this away-from-it-all space. I'm free to write thirty sentences that could open a novel, to look at all the archaic faces Piero della Francesca painted, to analyze the structure of a long poem. Or just to read a magazine in peace, or paint place cards for a party. Even when I am traveling or too busy, I love picturing those serene rooms waiting for me. Much about home is imagining home.

The structures scattered around the historic houses in town perhaps weren't all practical. I imagine a woman sorting garden seeds, writing in a diary, throwing clay pots, sewing for a mistress, writing a play, weaving on a loom, while in the main house life teems and swirls around her absence.

The path to the playhouse—take it.

My Southern Accent

*You can never go home again, but the truth is
you can never leave home so it's all right.*

—MAYA ANGELOU

❦

EVEN IF MY ACCENT SLIGHTLY DRIFTED DURING MY MANY years of living in California, New York, New Jersey, and Italy, I always said "y'all." Now, at home in North Carolina, it no longer provokes a smile. And once again, the cake is covered with icing, not frosting, there's dressing in the turkey, not stuffing, and I simply make slaw, not coleslaw. Caramel gets its middle "a" back and I don't have to hear the grating "kar-mul," or "pee-can" for "pee-kahn." When the lemon pie comes to the table, I can ask "What does this pie and my hand have in common?" And I know my daughter will call out "Mah rang!" Though I won't take up "that there," or "this here," or "might could," or even "bless your heart," I like hearing them. Southerners know that "bless your heart" isn't always sugar sweet; often it drips with irony.

I've always loved the southern accents, each one. Now that I'm living back in the South, my own Georgia pitch and rhythm becomes more pronounced as I recall the useful "fixin' to," "yonder," and "reckon." "Fixin' to" adds a dynamic that "about to" doesn't have; "yonder" just sounds farther than "over there"; and "reckon" adds a certain summing-up note of judgment that "think" doesn't give. "Y'all" has the same talent. While "you" acts as an ambiguous one or many, "y'all" is plural and an excellent clarifier. If I invite "you" to dinner, you might not know I mean to include the whole clan. "Y'all come to dinner" is precise in meaning. I even like "all y'all," the ultimate inclusive you.

In my early peregrinations, responses to my accent varied. We girls jumping on trains up to Princeton and Annapolis parties from the women's colleges in Virginia were surprised at the power we wielded. On those snowy weekends, the blind dates we met simply melted. They must have been dreaming in stereotypes of humid nights on some bayou, orange blossoms on the breeze, bees burrowing into the hibiscus flowers.

When the trips became frequent, my grandfather forbade me to go. He didn't want me "to marry some Yankee two-by-four, most common of all pieces of wood." Later, in accent-less California, I felt exotic but a few laid-back classmates at first looked at me as though I came from three generations of intermarriage with second cousins. Moving to New York for my husband's job, I was taken aback when his boss greeted me warmly, then, slightly into the conversation, asked with a smile, "Well, Miss Peaches, will you be enrolling in speech therapy?" I'd noted his harsh, nasal accent. "Why, no." I answered in a cane syrup drawl, "Will you?"

———

OUTSIDE OF THE SOUTH, we know we're often typecast as racist or dumb as a box of rocks the minute we open our mouths. Those stereotyping boors are unaware that we might be doing some fancy judging, too. I recall Lewis Grizzard, the 1970s Atlanta humorist, brutally observed that New York accents were "The most effective form of birth control . . ." Recently I came across an article written by a transplanted Chicago woman in Charlotte who worried about her three-year-old acquiring a southern accent. In the comments section, a responder to her said he didn't fit in up in Michigan because people told him his southern accent sounded terrible. "So, I told them they sound like a dyin' possum in a trash can." My parents had one New York friend who came to visit. At eight, I recall, I made fun of him in the kitchen because although my mother called him refined, he still said "dwahg" instead of "dawg," "ideers" for "ideas," and he pronounced Miami "Mee ah' me." I got switched on the legs.

MOSTLY, I'VE LOVED THE personal benefits of a southern accent. I thrill to the sound of a modulated voice with more soft notes than a harp. Etymologically, the root word of *accent* means "song." Although some twangy accents rake across your ears, most are melodious. How many instant connections have I found? Even a sense of community in far-flung places. I hear at the next table at a trattoria in Rome the lilt and sass of a southern accent drifting my way. Before the waiter pours the wine, it's a "Hey" and a "Where are you from?"

and before long I know where her mother grew up, and what cousin went to Emory, and that Daddy was a car dealer in Gainesville. In the dentist's chair in San Francisco, the hygienist says, "Do I detect a southern accent? I'm from Greenville, South Carolina, originally." She hadn't sounded like it before but immediately lapsed into her real voice. (Code switching is common in displaced southerners: Cover up your accent with a neutral voice.) She gouges my gums with her pointy instruments, regaling me with stories of crazy relatives. "You need to flawss more," she concludes. I relish these bonds. That a cadence provokes a link. The dropped *g* or *r* (goin', ov-ah), or a shifted emphasis (BE-hind, THANKS-giving, the-ATER), or run-together words—*atall* is one word—all signal home.

Accents are fading. Influxes of people from elsewhere, media rigidity favoring bland voices, the fear of being subjected to stereotyping—all these erode regional differences. People are sensitive to the possibility of a southern accent impacting their careers. Wait. Anyone think Molly Ivins, Truman Capote, or Tom Wolfe a bit dim? Dolly Parton or Morgan Freeman? Sam Ervin, the famous "law-yah" in the Watergate hearings? If so, you were shortly eviscerated by his rapier-sharp questioning. And the presidents Johnson, Carter, Bush, Clinton. Their panoply of local accents didn't stop them. Won't it be sad when we all sound as though we're computer generated? "Say riv-ah," I tell my grandson, but he won't. His teachers and friends in this Triangle area speak no Southern and most probably he never will either. There's nothing to do about this. I'm happy that the country is vast, with deeply defined regions and pockets and crannies and

mountaintops. We'll hold on to our heritages as far as we can
see.

Learning Italian, I began to hear the differences between
the Tuscans and the Venetians, the Neapolitans and the Sar-
dinians. I was delighted to be acquiring an accent in a language I barely could speak. It meant I was from Cortona, my
adopted hometown. I love the clackety sounds in Venice, the
lightning speed and elisions of Sicily, and the posh French-
ified sounds of the rich Piedmont region. I gradually was
loosened from my belief that if the angels came down to earth
they spoke Southern. I fell in love with accents, all kinds.
They belong to a place and time. And thereby the place belongs to the speaker of that accent. My husband's Minnesota
relatives sound as though they have snowflakes in their words.
Flinty fields appear in the Vermonters' voices, and old ballad
rhythms linger in the tumbling Appalachian waterfall of vow-
els. In "I Hear America Singing," Walt Whitman wrote:
"Each singing what belongs to him or her and to none else."
(And bless his heart—there, I said it—for including "her"
back in the 1860s.) I like what belongs to me and mine, but
why not celebrate differences? You say "motorcycle," and I
say "motah-sickle." Let's go for a ride.

The Ghost Who Cooks

Like other insomniacs I know, for me the blank, dark hours populate with visions of fast-proliferating brain tumors that burst, car crashes involving loved ones, a knife-wielding shadow creeping under the window, mice in the car vents, money squandered, an earthquake swaying the house and shaking the fillings out of my teeth.

Afflicted since childhood, I've devised coping strategies. I walk through all the homes I've lived in. Slowly, every room, every house. Tour my first herb garden. The lemon tree walk in Marin, the wild grasses with Mount Tamalpais in the distance. I swim in a green, languid river. I visit Istanbul and Crete, retracing what intrigued me. Calming, soporific journeys, all to lure elusive sleep.

"I didn't sleep at all," I tell Ed.

"You did. I woke up twice and you were sleeping."

"I did not. I was awake until six."

Insomnia is mysterious because it involves wake-sleep, a floating, interim level of consciousness, named evocatively in French: *dorveille,* from *dormir,* to sleep, and *veiller,* to be awake. Sometimes it's creative. I've solved plot issues, what car to buy, the layout of flower beds. I open the bedside table drawer and jot down ideas. Occasionally they're good ones, but mostly they make no sense the next morning. I count owl calls. I flip the pillow to the cool side.

Our bedroom at Chatwood has a wall of small-paned windows, a boon to sleeplessness. I can look out at clouds scudding across the moon and at shadows of branches, sharp as black ink calligraphy, writing across the floor. The room connects to a back stairway down to the living room, which joins a hallway leading to the kitchen.

Who believes in ghosts? Not me. When someone starts telling me about her father who was absolutely visited by a spirit, I tune out. When a novel I started reading began with a ghost, I shut it after four pages. The filmy presence in the attic—oh, please. That's a yellowed wedding dress. Ghost sightings are worse than hearing someone's dreams. I could walk through a cemetery at night. Halloween seems annoying at best.

But. It's three A.M. I've tossed. Pressed the clock ten times to check the hour. I'm remembering the opening of Proust's *Remembrance of Things Past*, how the boy longed for his mother, quickly shifting to yesterday afternoon, when we swam and floated on noodles with glasses of wine, talking about trips. The new Colette roses arrived. Time to plant. Focus on what soothes.

Then rises from the kitchen the aroma of—what—my pasta with four cheeses and sausage, drifting through the hall, up the stairs. I can almost separate the smells of the melting cheeses—ricotta, Parmigiano, mozzarella, taleggio. As often happens in insomniac nights, suddenly I'm not sure where I am. Is the scent drifting up the stairwell in Tuscany? I'm dreaming, I think. I know from Ed's minestrone that kitchen scents waft this far. I imagine setting the kitchen table for four. Candles, a jar of zinnias. But no. I'm awake. The oven-baked pasta, a vigorous smell.

I toss back the covers and creep to the door. The savory sausage, toasty crumbs. Feeling my way downstairs—third step from the bottom creaks—through the living room, into the hall, the house is silent. How silent inside a tomb must be. Who would not want out? At the kitchen door, I flick on the light. No bubbling, no oven door ajar. Nothing. No whoosh of a diaphanous white disappearance. The cold stove. The aroma? Gone.

Back in bed. I try to smell the moonlight but there's only my white cat, curled onto my pillow, Ed in whatever dreamland he's inhabiting. He sleeps hard, as if determined to sleep. How strange, sleep. How to fall asleep. To sleep, one falls. Come sleep, come now, I ask. Banquo, the ghost of Christmases past, the *Lincoln in the Bardo* spirits—even in literature, no haint comes back to cook.

One night a week later, also a Sunday: a whiff of lemon. Citrus? My sister's lemon pound cake. Maybe my friend's lemon-and-lime pasta with rosemary dust. I nudge Ed. "Do you smell something?" He sits up. "Fire?"

"No, the citrus pasta. Maybe pound cake."

"What? You're dreaming. Go back to sleep."

DOWN THE STAIRS I went. Through the living room, across the hall, into the fully lit kitchen. We'd forgotten to turn off the lights? No tangy citrus perfume. No cake rising, no pasta pot boiling. I opened the fridge, and the white glow shone in the opposite window, where no incandescent face looked in from beyond the beyond. I met my own gauzy reflection as I splashed my face with cold water at the copper sink.

IN OLD HOUSES, I sense the presence of those who lived there before me. Their chores, baptisms, deaths, graduations, all the milestones dwell in the walls. But no ghosts, ever. Now there's a ghost. One who comes home to cook. What will she serve forth tomorrow night to lure me downstairs? I'd come down for biscuits. Is there a story to hear? Will I come down every Sunday night? I'd come for scrambled eggs on toast. Pass the pepper. Or if my ghost is ambitious, a chocolate soufflé served with spoonfuls of crème anglaise. At that point, maybe she will appear, ready to talk.

She paid one more visit. I'd left a bowl of tomatoes on the counter, and in the deep night I smelled the hearty aroma of my own tomato sauce with a cup of herbs. I did not creep downstairs, because I knew the kitchen would be as spotless as I'd left it. Who understands the creative process, how ideas launch and where they come from? What you know before you know that you know. A few weeks later, I found myself writing a proposal for a pasta cookbook, all the fast pastas I've brought home from Italy to my own kitchen. Sister ghost got to the stove first, salting the pasta water, sending the tantalizing prospects gently up the stairs.

II

YEARNING
FOR
THE SUN

TOWARD THE APENNINES, TOWARD THE LAKE

*We would like only, for once, to get
to where we are already.*

—MARTIN HEIDEGGER

MY TUSCAN HOUSE FACES SOUTHEAST, POISED HIGH OVER a road lined with cypress trees. The facade looks down into a sweep of valley, toward the foothills of the Apennines and distant Lago Trasimeno, where Hannibal defeated the Romans in 217 B.C. I'm amazed at how often Hannibal comes up in daily conversation around here—previously, I had not heard him mentioned since World History in eighth grade. Now I know the weather conditions (foggy) on the morning of battle, the pass he took over the Alps en route to Rome, the number of elephants—he was down to only one—that he'd lost an eye, even what the Roman soldiers wore as they were driven into the misty lake and drowned.

Since I grew up in the American South—where hardly a day went by without a mention of the Civil War, some dim relative's elderberry wine, the Depression, or dead Aunt Besta's bread-and-butter pickles, or Uncle Jack spending his navy years during World War II cavorting in San Francisco—I'm used to the past layering onto the present. However,

217 B.C. lies beyond the reaches of memory of even the most indefatigable old bores. Hannibal is only the beginning, because in Tuscany, the past seems eternally present. I'm driving with a friend, and she points out the villa of a friend of hers, "That's where Luca Signorelli died when he stepped backward on the scaffolding to get a better perspective on his fresco." She speaks as though recalling a painter's unfortunate accident last year, not the Signorelli who died in 1523.

I wonder if this is why I came here, why I felt so instantly at home in Tuscany, when I have not a drop of blood from the Mediterranean world. Art lasts, in story and in fact. Faulkner's line "The past is never dead. It's not even past" comes as no revelation.

Cortona remains essentially medieval, with layers that peel back to pre-Etruscan times. Farmers turn up small bronze votive figures in their furrows and take them to the local Etruscan museum, where they're dated to the sixth century B.C. At the same time, the Jovanotti rock concert on a summer evening draws thousands to the parking area in front of the church, where the incorruptible body of Margherita of Cortona (rap-rock pulsating in her bones?) has lain since the thirteenth century. She's behind glass in her striped dress. Shops thrive in dark twelfth-century rabbit warrens with glass fronts, the owners perched on chairs in sunlight outside the doors.

In 1990, buying a house in a foreign country was drastic. Hardly any Americans rented houses here, and no one I ever heard of bought run-down Italian property. The end of my long marriage seemed to return me to a more audacious self, the adventurer I was in my youth. When the fur from the divorce settled, I found myself with a full-time job, my daughter in college, a modest stash of our stocks, my part of the sale of our home, and a new life to invent.

I was in no hurry, but I had a clear desire to transform those static blue chips into something pleasurable—a house with land. I heard the long echo of my grandfather saying, "Buy land, they aren't making it anymore."

As I have written in other books, I began to vacation in Italy. I'd always loved Italy, the food, landscape, perched villages, the great repository of art. Surely, I thought, it's an adequate substitute for just one man. Because I was teaching poetry at a university, I had three months off—my cherished writing time. For five summers, I rented farmhouses all over Tuscany. The first one, which I took for a month with Ed, new to me then, and two other writer friends, was outside Cortona. I'd found a listing in the little column *The New York Review of Books* ran for professors seeking research havens for sabbaticals. The thrifty English writer's country house was bare. The four upstairs rooms had lumpy, damp beds and rickety chests. Inside the drawers I found pyramids of ground-up wood. *Tarli,* a woman from the farm across the field explained. I've never known what *tarli* are, only what they do. The living room was furnished with cheap bamboo. We didn't care. The woman, Annette, stopped by often, dropping off eggs and armfuls of wildflowers. I remember the blue bowl of soft teal, malt, and ivory eggs, the weedy flowers, and her raucous laugh at our pitiful attempt to roll out fresh pasta on the worn worktable in the kitchen. Annette taught us that even our irregular pieces had a name, *maltagliata,* badly cut, and were still very good. We chopped and quoted Rilke and danced. I loved these friends, C. D. Wright and Forrest Gander. (Both went on to become important poets.) We were all four charged with that rustling awareness of possibility. There's a bond to make with a few people, close to a sense of family—but chosen family. Carolyn, although from Arkansas, had an accent similar to mine. We spent mornings interviewing each other about women writers and memoir and childhood. Always audacious, Carolyn came downstairs one evening as Ed and I chopped vegetables. Forrest was still up in their room. Pausing at the foot of the stairs, she announced, "I am freshly fucked and childless." We swam in the priest's icy spring-fed pool, gossiping because the priest had a girlfriend.

I had just finished writing *The Discovery of Poetry,* a 500-page poetry textbook, and didn't care if I ever wrote another word. They worked; I read guidebooks and made lunch, then dragged them to one hot hill town after another, ending up at some wonderful restaurant for a long dinner. I saw that Ed's attitude toward life was romantic. He was the ideal traveler, lover, writer. We read poetry aloud under an olive tree. Norwegian friends from Princeton days came to stay. A poet from Rome whose translations we knew popped in, along with Gail Tsukiyama, who became a novelist but was then a student of mine. From across the field at night came the plaintive music of Bruno's accordion as we sat around a fire, outdoing each other with revelations and quotes and flashes of wit. When the fire died down, we had the outrageous Milky Way to teach us a thing or two.

All this remains memorable, but it was something else that skewed the course of my life.

In the distance a tumbledown farmhouse drew me on afternoon walks. The stone outlines of pigpens set me thinking of small studios for writing. The arch for wagons to enter the downstairs would, I saw, nicely transform into a living room window. The deep pleasures of county life. I thought, *How can I have that?* A first inkling. A chance image can turn your life around. I planted basil the first day there, and by the end of the month, the plants were knee-high. I was rooted, too.

Summers after that, I tried Montisi, Florence, Quercegrossa, Rignano sul Arno, Volterra, Siena, Vicchio—two weeks here, a month there, savoring different areas, always with Ed. (Our friends did not come back.) Always, I was drawn to Cortona, to my first impressions of the tawny old houses placed as though by a large hand on the hilltops, and the bells of Cortona's thirty-odd churches ringing over the fields, reverberating in the bones of my head. I thought that here I would begin to write poems and essays not in the usual way, on legal pads and computer (primitive then), but with a pen, real ink, in one of those handmade marbled books, a big one, with thick, creamy paper.

That fifth summer, I began to look seriously at houses. Because I was by then establishing a permanent relationship with both Ed and Italy, the house quest felt tied to whatever patterns we would create in the future. Ed had no idea that our shared interest in literature would shift so soon to titles such as *The Home Water Supply* and *The Complete Guide to Plastering*.

I was no longer amused at the caprices of renting the greatly charming country houses: sagging beds or kitchens with no hot water, or bats roosting in fireplaces. The quirks were fun at first. The place I rented in Vinci had an odd kitchen current. Every time I touched an appliance, I got a tingling jolt. The refrigerator's freezer compartment formed an igloo every two days so that I couldn't shut the door. When it rained, the caretaker flew through the rooms shrieking and banging shutters, oblivious to my state of dress or undress. My daughter, friends who came to visit, and Ed drove with me over back roads that turned into paths, discussed how cow mangers could be turned into banquettes, and cooled my enthusiasm when one enchanting place had no road in at all and a family of black snakes guarded the threshold. We found several houses to love but Tuscans hate to part with property and owners often changed their minds. One ancient contessa cried to think of selling, doubled her price, and seemed cheered as we walked away. This scene later appeared almost verbatim in the movie *Under the Tuscan Sun*. By now, almost all those roughly authentic farmhouses are restored to the hilt. Comfort and style gained, purity and romance often lost.

Before I saw my house, I'd given up. I was leaving in two days, had thanked the local agent and said goodbye. The next morning, I ran into him in the piazza. He hustled me toward his Fiat. His limp gone, he sprinted, shouting, "A house with the beautiful name Bramasole." I didn't catch much else of what he said other than "*il disastro*."

This is the story I've told in other books and many speeches, yet it always seems a new discovery when I remember it. Out of Cortona, he took the uphill road that climbs toward Città di Castello. At the *località* Torreone, he turned onto a *strada bianca* (white road) and, after a kilometer, pulled into a sloping driveway. I caught a glimpse of a shrine with a ceramic Madonna then looked up at a tall, faded gold house with green shutters, a balcony, and rambling overgrown bushes and briars. I was restless as we drove up. "Perfect, I'll take it," I joked when we got out. Rusty iron arches created a tunnel for climbing roses. A frog as big as my foot guarded the cistern in a fallen stone wall. I loved the curly fanlight over the double door with two sphinx knockers. The sphinx motif, I'd read, was popular when Mussolini was trying to lay claim to African countries. The house's walls were as thick as my arm is long, longer! Almost iridescent, glass in the windows quivered with light. I scuffed through silty dust and saw intact *cotto* (old brick) floors crusty with dirt. He showed me two bathrooms, alarming—I'd never heard of bucket flush— but functioning, after all the houses I'd seen with no water, much less plumbing. No one had lived in the house for thirty years and the five acres seemed enchanted, rampant with weeds, dog roses, and blackberries. Ivy twisted into trees and ran over fallen stone walls. Ivy will survive nuclear blasts.

Anselmo, the agent, shielded his eyes and surveyed the land. "*Molto lavoro,*" he pronounced, much work. Also, something that must have meant *You'd be out of your gourd to take on this baby.* (Italian agents in my experience never try to sell.)

"It's unbelievably romantic," I answered. Within five minutes, I envisioned snipping sun-warmed thyme and oregano into a basket over my arm, setting a long table with checked cloth under the linden trees, Ed grilling chops in the big fireplace. I simply wanted to hang my linen dresses on a peg and stack my notebooks under a window looking out at the six hundred cypresses bordering the road, each one planted for a boy who died in World War I.

After summers of looking at houses situated on the Arno's floodplains or ones with collapsed roofs, or, worse, ludicrous restorations, after miles of dusty roads, this house seemed to have been waiting all along.

THE GREAT OLD TUSCAN sun pouring into every room warmed me. There's something beneficent about the Italian sun; it seems to seep farther in, gently freeing the blood and the mind. I felt renewed, excited, and calmly right, and I suppose that's the real sensation of feeling at home in the world.

In the United States, I've bought and sold houses before— loaded up the car with the blue-and-white Wedgwood, the cat, and the fichus for the three-mile or three-thousand-mile drive to the next doorway, where a new key would fit. Choices were practical, bound to graduate schools, or jobs, or worse, divorce. But this time the new door's iron key weighed half a pound; the doorway was seven thousand miles from home. The legal language and the baroque arrangements of buying baffled me. Currency rates were falling, then rising. My financial advisor was selling my life savings and gently chiding me about la dolce vita. (Later he told me he was 100 percent behind me.) I can still wake up thinking, what on earth have you done and why, when you could have had a cottage on the California coast where you could buzz up for the weekend, the back seat full of groceries, could plant bulbs at the proper moment and easily see about broken pipes. I'd looked for a place in Sonoma, even made an offer and was instructed by how relieved I felt when it was turned down.

The hitch—I already knew what to expect from my California environs. I considered my home state, Georgia. I love the barrier islands where I spent summers as a child. A white board house with a porch always represents the quintessential image of home. But I was running on instinct, and instinct said time for a new kind of home. Why not, in middle age, remember Dante's dilemma: What now to do in order to grow? I wanted the unknown, wanted to do something I didn't know how to do (and didn't I get my wish!). Italy always had a magnetic allure. No matter how long I spend here, I never will resist turning off the road to explore a walled hill town, a local Saturday market, or a country Romanesque church where I might find a Masaccio triptych or an austere fresco by some unknown hand. Language, art, cuisine, literature, and beauty: Everything attracts me.

My little villa made of stones stands on a terraced hillside covered with olive trees. Close to the house, some kindly soul planted fruit and nut trees—apricot, fig, plum, apple, hazelnut, almond, and many kinds of pears, which bear in sequence so that from summer through late fall I find pears to pick and a reason to stock the kitchen with gorgonzola. A neighbor said, "Your house is only a few hundred years old—mine is a thousand." He's right, the house, started in the 1700s, is not old by local standards. Although I admire the type of stone farmhouse called *casa colonica*, I did not end up buying one; nor is mine a real villa. Although there are fourteen rooms, none has the ample proportions of a house of the nobility. The early builder might have been eager to leave behind the

memory of some dank stone farmhouse of his childhood, because he had his stones gentrified with a stucco facing. Over
the years, the various coats of paint wore away at different
speeds so that the house, now predominantly luxurious apricot, reveals its rosy phase and its time as a vivid yellow. Lichen traces splotchy signatures of black and green. When
winter light hits the facade, the house looks bleached and lem-
ony. When summer rain soaks in, the walls turn the color of a
blood orange. On bright days, it might have been painted by
an amateur watercolorist who imitated flagrant sunrises. The
surface bothers the Italian builders I've since had in for several restoration projects. "Completely replaster, signora,
paint it gold," they advise. "You need to start over—it will
look like new." When I say I love the color, they look sad. But
I'm an American, full of strange caprices and to be indulged
like a spoiled child.

The symmetrical house rises three stories, with the fanciful iron balcony on the second floor above the double front
door. From it, I train hanging pink Mandeville vines and geraniums, but I imagine someone once stepping out to hear a
lover sing "Ecco Maggio," or something equally corny. I
bought the place from a doctor, who recently had acquired it
from five siblings from Perugia. The five linden trees in a row
were named for the children when their father planted them
years ago. The doctor thought to make it a summer home then
changed his mind. It is not he, because he never lived here,
but the five children I think of often. They were four girls,
who must have simultaneously pushed open the shutters of
their five bedrooms and leaned out in their white nightgowns.
The boy must have escaped them, trapping fireflies in a jar.

Such are the kinds of rumination the house inspires. Why? Because it is a dream house. Not a dream house in the sense that it has the perfect proportions and the ideal floor plan— and I don't think dream houses have albino scorpions in the bidet—but more that it resembles a house from a dream, one of those where you discover a room you did not know existed and in it a dry plant breaks into full bloom, or you come upon it alone, lights blazing in all the windows, and you see yourself in every room. Here, I dream recurrently of swimming without effort in a clear green river, totally at home in the water, buoyantly carried downstream with the flow.

I'm dazzled by the remains of a Roman road over the hill covered with wildflowers. I follow that stony path through the poppies into Cortona for espresso. I'm dazzled by the old cistern with a brick archway underground. Secret passage? The caretaker at the Medici fortress up above claims an underground escape route goes downhill to the valley, then to the lake. Italians take such remains casually; that one is allowed to own such ancient things seems preposterous to me. I'm dazzled, period.

Two improbably tall palms grew on the terrace in front of the house. They clattered gently just under the third-floor window. One friend said, "Cut down those things; they look decadent, like something out of that old movie *Last Year at Marienbad*." Italians marvel: that they've grown tall means that the house is in a microclimate. Finally, one palm died, leaving the other to asymmetrically punctuate the front of the house. I go for the tropical accent, as though the house could be in Tunisia or Sardinia as easily as here. Even the roof ranks among the extraordinary discoveries of the every day. I climb up the terraces and look down on the old tiles, formed over someone's knee and now alive with lacy gray moss. What else? The *cotto* floors, once scrubbed, have been polished by enough rags over the years that even the quickest mopping makes them glow.

We bottle our own olive oil now, but I used to like the deeply satisfying tilt of the demijohn as I drew off enough for the day's cooking. All these, yes, and the cool marble counters where the semolina gnocchi never stick; the small owl that perches on a windowsill and looks in, where on one bedroom's walls, a friend painted blue domes over the windows and filled them with Giotto-like gold stars (I marvel that though she has since died, her stars remain as fresh as ever). Some of them escape the dome and fall down the white walls. During dramatic storms, thunder seems to rearrange the stones in the walls. The straight-up stairs have a wrought-iron railing that kept some *fabbro*, blacksmith, busy an entire winter. Ed stripped and waxed each room's chestnut beams. Some genius had slathered all of them with a sticky mud-colored veneer. We discovered that all the bedrooms had fanciful designs on the walls. We've left "truth windows" that let me imagine what the whole room of lattice and flowers must have looked like, or borders of acanthus, broad blue stripes, and in one, just recently uncovered, drawn-back coral brocade-edged draperies that must have focused the eye on a bed. Everything painted! Which must have lightened the heavy chestnut furniture that furnished these homes. Windows are bare, except for their intricate layers of louvered, solid, and glassed shutters.

At least once a day, I go out on the second-floor patio and

look up the hill where the terraces stop. I can see a section of Etruscan wall that has the exact orientation as the house. If the wall had not securely kept vigil over this land for twenty-six centuries, I would be afraid it might tumble on us one day. Blocks of stone as big as Hannibal's elephants. Blocks on blocks. This Etruscan wall forms part of Cortona's original town wall. A couple of Etruscan gates and tombs remain scattered about. But this section of wall is different. From its position, historians think it is a remnant of a sun temple. The name of my house, Bramasole, comes from *bramare*, "to yearn for," and *sole*, "sun": Something that yearns for the sun. I've always been surprised that everyone knows this house. *"Ah, Bramasole, sì, una bella casa,"* they say. Delivery people, even from miles away, do not need a map, *"Sì, sì, la villa Bramasole,"* they say. They or their parents picked cherries or nuts here during its abandoned thirty years, or even earlier. They've gathered mistletoe from the almond trees at Christmas. Their grandmother picked figs every September. A friend's father was blown to bits after World War II when he unearthed a pipe that turned out to be a German land mine.

I thought it was just a house everyone knew. One day in town I spotted a postcard of the Etruscan wall. It was identified as being in "the locality Bramasole." I discovered the name of the land is much older than my house. Possibly "Bramasole" connects to the ancient purpose of this site, the lost temple where people like me came when they were yearning for the sun.

DINNER / CENA

WHEN I FIRST STARTED COOKING AT BRAMASOLE, I LOVED the heightened flavors and simplicity of local food. I felt at home with the plenitude and hospitality I found at the Italian table—so close to my southern traditions. No one need explain why Italian is the one cuisine you see all over the world. Easy to love, the food remains intensely diverse from north to south. As I made friends and began to dine at their houses and invite them over to mine, my whole approach to cooking changed.

I grew up in a family who talked at midday dinner about what was for dinner tomorrow. I liked to sit on the counter ("Don't kick those cabinet doors!"), dip a spoon into a bowl of potato salad, or help top and tail green beans. I watched all the preparations, but I didn't want to touch raw meat or chicken. I would help a little with the baking—melting chocolate and butter together but no cracking of creepy eggs.

Once grown with no one to cook for me, I reveled in chopping, shredding, braising, whipping. I launched into trying my mother's recipes. A few years later, I cooked my way through Julia Child. I studied French cuisine with Julia's co-author Simone Beck in Provence. I took courses in Chinese,

Mexican, and Moroccan cooking. Cooking was fun but time-consuming, the meal gone faster than the time I spent making it.

In Italy, I noticed that my neighbors entertained on weeknights, leaving their jobs at five or six and managing dinner for a few friends at eight. That was a revelation. For most dinner parties, I usually cooked for two days. Leave it to the Italians—their recipes cut through the labor-intensive parts and go straight to the flavor. How simple, for example, is a caprese? With prime ingredients (that's the secret), only ripe tomatoes, Genovese basil, buffalo mozzarella, you have a genius salad exquisitely balanced, beautiful to see, and so quick.

Everything about cooking seemed different. It was like waking up with a new husband. (Which I'd also done!) In Italian friends' kitchens, there is little equipment, compared with my American array of everything from avocado cutters to pineapple corers to spiralizers. Divine meals appear without the aid of immersion blenders, food processors, mandolines, heavyweight pans, slow cookers, air fryers, instant pots, even measuring spoons and cups. (I have never seen measuring spoons for sale in Italy.) Stoves are usually just standard-issue stoves, and refrigerators are at most half the size of mine at home. Only now in rural Tuscany are dishwashers becoming the norm. Could this simplification of the kitchen have something to do with the ease of preparing the Tuscan repertoire? Is the pared-down kitchen better?

I saw a parallel with ingredients. Fresh extra-virgin olive oil is the baseline of Tuscan cooking; the fruity elixir transforms whatever it's sprinkled or poured over. What luck, to harvest our own oil. By now, I've eliminated 90 percent of the butter I used to use, and my flavors are better. My pantry at home in the States had seven vinegars, a stock of food that would serve me well in a snowstorm, dozens of jars of fancy preserves, goat milk caramel spread, peppered peanuts, canisters of beans and grains, and jars mysteriously hidden behind odd ingredients such as pecan flour and my husband's collection of fancy oatmeals, if that's not an oxymoron.

Instead, in my friend Domenica's *dispensa,* shelves are lined with jars of put-up tomatoes, each with a basil sprig showing at the top. How many? About three hundred. Other bounty of summer gleams like jewels—jars of golden peaches, plums like garnets, eggplants dark as onyx, roasted red peppers, tawny fennel seeds, capers, and the whole panoply of fruit jams ready for the ubiquitous fruit tart, the crostata. A white cloth covers a prosciutto lodged in its special rack; *salume* hang from nails, ready for the antipasto plate.

Ah, that's why dinner is so quick! Reach for the dried mushrooms and tomatoes. Pasta's ready. Roll out pastry, spread on the jam, lattice the top, and the crostata is done, that dessert you have loved since you were two. I learned the necessity of a large vegetable garden, the bartering of melons and squash, the payoff of peeling all those tomatoes and scalding the jars.

My friends grow their own herbs and use them copiously. I recently saw a recipe from an American chef that called for a tablespoon of basil. That's exactly what I've learned not to do in Italy. What is a tablespoon? Two leaves, three? And how do you even measure basil onto a tablespoon? My use of herbs quadrupled, and I don't mix many together. Why muddle the tastes? A favorite pasta with tomato sauce has a couple of big handfuls of parsley and basil stirred in at the end. Delicious. I also adapted to their much-adored *peperoncini,* hot pepper flakes. Italian tables hold no salt and pepper (since the food is already seasoned), but you inevitably see a shaker of home-grown red pepper passed around so everyone can add fire to taste. Beware!

We Americans are big on grilling outside, as are the Tuscans. In cold weather, though, the action shifts inside. Everyone cooks in the fireplace. When we were first there, spring-loaded rotisseries were hand-cranked but now most are electric, slowly spinning a guinea hen, sausages, and hunks of pork liver. I love what this does to the atmosphere of a kitchen or dining room—those succulent aromas surrounding the table where you soon will draw up a chair. Although in our fireplace we venture only as far as veal chops and skewers of shrimp or chicken, we frequently use, as most country Italian families do, a long-handled chestnut roaster. There's nothing more contemplative than peeling floury, hot chestnuts and savoring the ancient taste of the forest. Evenings by the fire, the plates pushed aside, the good red poured—the best recipe of all.

I love my southern desserts, especially pecan pie, caramel cake, and coconut cake. I was excited to share them with my friends in Italy. "Oh, so sweet!" Daria exclaimed, mouth puckered, barely able to speak. Other guests just take a polite couple of bites. Although I always love their food—well, not those gristly veal knuckles—they don't always love the American desserts. Tuscan desserts are not sweet, one of many vast cultural differences. My cake has three cups of sugar. Gilda's has one. Even the crostata isn't sweet, since no sugar is added to the fruit jams. Which do I prefer? Hands down, the loaded southern desserts. Now that weight recently has entered my mind, I do try to reach for the tangerines after dinner, the walnuts to crack, or even bone-dry biscotti so hard they could split a tooth. I wish cooking in Italy had not made me so conscious of sugar. I used to enjoy my brownie and Coke so much.

Italians believe that their nonna knew best; it's her ragù they crave. Even when they travel, my Tuscan friends long for the food of home. Often, they take along a few cans of *pelati,* tomatoes, for an emergency pasta. Your food is your culture. How can anything compare? Long away from my native shore, I'll bake that pan of chocolate chip cookies, or whip up pancakes for Sunday breakfast. I won't forget when I caught a dear Tuscan neighbor who was visiting me. She was up at two A.M. in the kitchen preparing pasta and tomato sauce. This after my proud feast of shrimp and grits, Brunswick stew, and my grandmother's mile-high coconut pie. "So interesting," she'd remarked as she set down her fork.

Back in North Carolina, I love to have friends over once a week at least. (I'm still not up to the constant entertaining many Tuscans take for granted.) Gathered around a table, I'm attending a ritual. Each platter arrives with images of a grandmother, a mother, and with tastes and memories from hundreds of dinners with friends. With everyone relishing my Tuscan baked pasta with four cheeses, I'm happy. Or maybe I'm serving my aunt's southern ribs and roasted sweet potatoes, with chocolate chess pie for dessert. I'm serving, too, variations on themes, as cooks will do—surprise combinations and innovations that arise when I'm presented with a bunch of watermelon radishes or a bumper crop of chard. The excitement of cooking across two cultures keeps the kitchen vibrant. What you eat is who you were and are. When you cook the food you love most, you land at home.

TIME DIFFERENCE

I

THE SIX-HOUR TIME DIFFERENCE BETWEEN NORTH CAR-
olina and Tuscany permanently destroyed my circadian
rhythm. I wake up and glance at the time. Seven A.M. here,
and I know my Cortona neighbors are sitting down to lunch.
Eight P.M. here, time for dinner, and they're dreaming in their
beds. When I fly over, part of the night is lost into oblivion, so
that I emerge from the plane into the full Roman morning.
Fuso orario, fused, melted, smelted, worn-out hours? All
these, but the term translates "jet lag." To cure it, Italians tell
me, go stand in the sun.

Returning to the South, I take back that lost time, leveling
into Raleigh-Durham Airport on the tail end of a long, long
day. Living in two countries, absorbing their rhythms deeply,
creates parallel time. At odd moments in the day, I have the
disorienting experience of looking at the sun and feeling the
arc of its daily journey swoop through my head.

Living in Italy and the USA—how differently we live in
time. Italy mixes fast and slow. Motorcyclists seem to have a
death wish. "Dead by dark," I say to Ed on the autostrada as

a pack of them weaves in and out, taking the center line as a new lane. Ed speeds, too. "Italians are fast but expert," he maintains. "You don't venture into the left lane unless you're passing."

Slow? How puzzling the term "slow food." The term must have come from fear of fast food spreading to Italy. How slow can you go? A five-hour Sunday lunch has always been normal. Eight-hour feasts are not at all unknown. I've stumbled out of many, utterly deranged by umpteen courses and wines. We Americans are geared toward TGIF and weekend relaxation but for my Italian friends, any night will do. Even travelers feel it. They attribute this go-with-the-flow to la dolce vita, and it is. Behind that, however, there's something more profound, a way of living in time. No one at my university in San Francisco blinked when the building where I taught was scheduled to be demolished. The reason? It was fifty years old. Early on in Italy, I wrote: *Time is a river. Might as well float.*

Always striking to me is my American penchant for change versus the Italian ability to bring along the past into the present. After eight or ten years, I usually want to revise my rooms, if not move to another house. My Italian neighbors put their home together when they married forty years ago and haven't so much as moved the sofa to the other side of the room. This is Italy's gift—how to be at home in time. To be at home in time is to be at home in the world. (Meanwhile those two chairs in my living room were a mistake and have to go.)

How anciently sophisticated and resigned Italians are. Politics? They're all crooks. A fatalism, avoiding engagement because you're bound to be disappointed; don't rock any boat: The person you fight will seek revenge. In contrast, how perpetually innocent and expectant Americans are. Our belief in the new. Election after election. I prefer the optimism of my country.

Many Americans no longer feel as at home in their own country as they used to. The past few years made clear the divisions among us that rest on multitudes of failures and mistakes, as well as the understanding that we were never who we thought we were.

We turned cynical about politics, adopting irony on Twitter and, yes, biting, outrageous humor. At least we can still laugh. The rents in our national fabric became overstitched with clever digs, caricatures, jokes, parody. These cover a deeply disturbing sense of helplessness: There's money for the huge new jail but not enough for the third-grade teacher to supply pens and paper. Progress in environmental issues wrenched backwards. Who could be against clean water? Personally, we may recycle and cut back on plastic, but we cannot save the dirty oceans ourselves. I carefully snip the round disc in the top of the milk bottle so it doesn't choke a turtle when it makes its way to the ocean, as it will. Even my toothbrush will last a thousand years in a landfill. We rail against barbarian immigration practices and absurd wars. Vote! Donate! We do what we can and it's not nothing, but I'm hard put to think anything I can do will spark change. Temperatures are spiking all over the globe and fires come out of Armageddon. Italians are fatalistic but American fatalism—brutal, violent, illogical—has a different cast.

Every president runs on change. Each new president offers his version, and we are hopeful people.

In this new chaos, division, darkness, we lack the great leveler of a sense of time—an Italian heritage. We are not born with the time awareness that all Italians seem to have instinctively. They have long time behind them, eons of civilization, art, literature, humanism. A common culture to draw on, while America forgets as it goes. Humanism makes the current world more bearable. Italians live in their towns the way we Americans live in our houses. The piazza becomes a big living room and there you are, not hunched before a screen railing at Facebook, adding your vaporous opinions, but at least sitting under the old stars, among others.

2

WHEN THE COVID VIRUS struck Italy, it hit hard. In America, we were still in denial that it would reach us. From afar, I was amazed at how Italy pulled together, anarchistic as they are, physically expressive as they are, social and familial as they are. There was no nonsense. They fell to, mostly obeying the strictures placed upon them and enforced. There was little idiocy about not recognizing the virus for what it is. When America was hit, the opposite happened. Too many waved little *me* flags, refusing to give up their individual rights to spread as many germs as they wanted. The then-president concurred, and we all know the result.

While the Italians came out and sang on their balconies to one another, Americans stomped out to political rallies without masks. While the Italian banners read *Tutto andrà bene,* all will be well, and the informed people stayed home, our leader was proclaiming poof, it will be gone! We were urged by the media to lose weight, and to cut back on drinking to avoid "lockdown liver." Things turned surreal. We were advised to hold a séance, master the Tarot, collage our bathrooms. Insanity walked the land. Even in hospital beds, many of the seriously ill and dying refused to believe they had the virus. Why?

We will be analyzing the American response for years and frankly enough is enough: I won't be reading the articles. Wait, yes, I will. What happened is not the blip of a few paragraphs in future history books. It's monumental. Our descendants will be studying this period the way we studied the Spanish flu and the waves of plague, the Black Death that scourged Europe, Africa, Eurasia. From the mid-fourteenth century until well into the seventeenth, the *Britannica* tells me, an estimated 25 million Europeans died from *la pesta nera.*

Over my neighbor Placido's gate, he hung a gourd painted in the green, white, and red of the Italian flag with one word printed: *coraggio,* courage. People stayed at home for months. They were in it together. But we Americans, as a nation we've lost the concept of *in this together.*

I came back to Italy in the fall of 2020, as the coronavirus was staging a second rise. Everyone was tired but when the "orange" then the dreaded "red" rules hit, we all cooperated again. We were not permitted to leave town. We could still touch the omphalos, that navel of the universe, our home piazza, then line up at the *frutta e verdure,* the pharmacy, the post office, to enter one by one.

When I walked into the Porta Colonia and along via Dardano to take my allowed turn at the market, I always noticed Cortona's strange architectural remnants of the bubonic plague, the doors of the dead. Most of the doors have been bricked over but three remain intact. These odd narrow doors are raised about a yard from street level. As the story goes, during the plague the family risked more bad luck if they took a body out of the *portone,* the main door of the home. They could slide the corpse out the special opening, onto a cart, and goodbye to you. Chilling to think it took centuries to figure out the cause of the waves of plague—a bacteria in rats transferred to fleas, fleas to humans. Are the ancient plague doors why the local citizens comply with the modern plague rules? Because they remember? If you pass the strange doors, you have to feel a shiver.

At the end of the park, a pleasant residence with tall arched windows and a rose garden is still called Plague House. It is said that some victims were brought from their homes and dumped there to live or die, mostly the latter. I walk by and conjure lined-up pallets and bodies covered in festering buboes and the frightening doctor in that pointy-nose hooded garb that looks like a huge crow. I doubt if anyone then was counseled to keep a gratitude journal, take up Zumba, collage the bathroom, master the Tarot, or to *breathe,* as we often have been advised. Plant herbs. Make a playlist. Send a friend a thousand-piece puzzle.

In Italy, where time is long, these strange remaining structures serve as memento mori. The plague was centuries ago, but here are the filled-in doors and this spooky house to remind us daily. With such images residing in the collective memory, you entertain no nonsense about fastening that blue mask over your face as you walk out into a present-day plague. I pass a masked mother pointing at a door of the dead. Her little son looks up, wide-eyed, at the studded door as she leans down to explain.

Waves of plague broke Europe and much of the world and are recorded in the blood tides of those enduring this one. Time, a Möbius strip, a continuous surface that turns on itself. Italians own time and time owns them. Time difference, more than a matter of hours.

Risking Happiness

Happiness . . . not in another place but this place,
not for another hour but this hour.

—WALT WHITMAN

⚷

THE NIGHT BEFORE I BOUGHT AN ABANDONED HOUSE IN the Tuscan hills, I couldn't sleep. For one thing, the church bells near the hotel rang not only the hour but sent out a few bonus clangs for quarter and half hours as well. I was about to get rope burn from churning on rough cotton sheets. It was summer in Cortona, the driest July in memory. Even the night couldn't cool down stony streets torched all day by the fierce sun.

I sat up and wrote in my notebook, *I am about to buy a house in a foreign country. Why have I gotten myself into this? Make a list!* This is all I could come up with: It is so beautiful. The bells—four, five, six. And as we know from the poet John Donne, they toll for thee. Remembering that somber thought, I quickly scrawled in my notebook: *Carpe diem!* And *Why not?*

Though I still could have backed out, I made my way to the notary office the next day and listened to the endless contract read aloud in Italian. I didn't understand one word. The agent handed me a huge iron key and that was that.

Nothing ventured, nothing gained always made sense to me. I'd gone off to college far from home, set out for California after that, made a university teaching career in poetry, left a solid marriage for the lure of big romance. I'll take a risk. But I'd never taken a peculiar risk like this—plunking down my life savings on an abandoned house thousands of miles from home. I was single. No safety net. Everyone said I was insane to consider such a thing. "You'll live to regret this," a relative said. (Later, the relatives poured in for visits.)

No, I didn't. "What luck," I soon found myself writing. "What is this happiness that keeps coming in waves?"

Though never a major subject for philosophers, happiness preoccupies the rest of us all our lives. Hundreds of self-help books attempt to steer our thinking along positive paths. One advises: Keep an image journal, which seems like a good idea. On punishing diets, we're offered a "happy meal." Emails come to us decorated with the smiley face emoji and red hearts. Any time we're photographed we are urged to smile so that our happiness at that moment is verified. The right to the pursuit of happiness even anchors the U.S. Declaration of Independence. But happiness is elusive, and the "pursuit" of it sounds desperate, as if you must stalk it. I associated happiness with moments of surging joy—falling in love, birth of a child, starting a new manuscript, the plane taking off for Peru. All big moments, with the rest of life proceeding along, powered by a tailwind, with stretches of turbulence.

THE WAVES OF HAPPINESS I began to experience in Italy, however, came from seeing how easily my neighbors went about their days, and from living close to the seasons in a place of beauty. The rhythms of life assumed a natural pace, not the frenetic one I was used to. Many changes came quickly, and I can't sort out a quantitative cause and effect that catapulted me into a baseline happiness, but I came across a succinct quote from Aristotle: "Happiness belongs to the self-sufficient." Taking a risk means you are in charge of yourself; it builds a foundation under your feet. You literally seize the day. In my novel *Women in Sunlight,* three women set on a predicted path break away and change their lives. In the story, each comes upon a private moment of change, and each seizes that moment. For Julia, it's a leap off a cliff into the sea at Cinque Terre. I loved writing the scene because I gave her the feeling I always have when I have stepped up to an edge. At that moment, you own your life and the place you make for yourself.

I read one of my favorite Italian poets, Cesare Pavese: "The only joy in the world is to begin." Beginning a new life in a foreign country, beginning a journey, beginning a relationship, yes, those are joys, but so are the smaller beginnings on the other side of risk that sustain you on any random Wednesday.

I slipped into several. I began to simplify. I learned to cook the Italian way and my kitchen transformed. I came to think that once or twice a week is the right number of times to have friends over for dinner. I began to love bright packets of seeds. We raise a lot of our vegetables—what a pleasure. I walk over Roman roads listening to audio books, simply lost for long treks. To begin a new language causes brilliant sparks in the brain and even changes your dreams.

I began to build a nature photo album and notebook, to capture in an image or paragraph a wild spotted orange lily or an autumn tree glowing with persimmons, or a cloud like a load of sheets from the dryer. This isn't a book I'm writing, but a sort of meditation on the natural world. Without this habit, I would not have discovered the outlandish chartreuse-and-purple *bellavedova* (beautiful widow) iris growing on my hillside. My camera and pen keep me observant and connect me to stands of red poppies, tart wild plums, a field of heather, ethereal almond blossoms, and deadly poisonous mushrooms. The pleasure isn't at all like that of posting on Instagram. It's private and meditative.

I love beginning the day with a writer. I choose one for a whole month and give her each day a short, dedicated time of reading. I become an apprentice to a mind I admire. Recently, I've loved *The Stories of Jane Gardam*. Pages of play with language, subjects turned upside down and inside out, plus a quirky, rough sensibility that is often funny, risks the absurd without quite succumbing. She's my exciting companion for now.

As I began these devotions, an ancillary benefit occurred. One morning at breakfast I realized I was ingesting with my cappuccino and toast bad news—terrorism, riots, floating corpses in the Mississippi River. As I started to notice all the violence and fear I took in every day, I became allergic to the toxic effects of news. In my notes I wrote: Subtract a little media every day. Not that I advocate a head-in-the-sand mentality. I read news three or so times a week. Politics and world events are frequently discussed with friends. *Basta*. Enough. The news is bad. I don't want my daily bread with a dose of horror, especially when disaster strikes and is endlessly repeated, sometimes with relish. This reiteration simultaneously deadens you to the event and raises anxiety. Mayhem, murder, and monstrous acts give a sense of the world that is true but not all the truth. My friend Josephine said, "That's the wound of the world. Don't mistake the wound of the world with the world you know and love."

Tune out, tune in. Unfollow those Facebook zealots who get on your nerves; even cat videos on Instagram are better. Víkingur Ólafsson on the piano or Joshua Bell on the violin or Yo-Yo Ma on the cello will justify the world every morning, raising your natural exhilaration and zest, rather than weighing the bloodstream with lead.

Acting on an irrational desire that arises from some deep place may be one of the best decisions you make in your life. For me, the strength behind taking a risk emanates from a gold locket I wore as a child. This locket opens to a picture of my mother, who did not have the chance to do many of the things that I do. As a decision approaches, I snap open the locket, which no longer actually exists. There's her pretty face looking at me. *Go,* she whispers. *Yes! Go!*

In the study of the house I did not live to regret, I recently began writing a new book. The first line came to me. A line I think can take me to the end. At this desk I sit down to a plethora of words, images, story. Through the window open to a view of hills, I hear the deep gongs of bells over Cortona marking time, what luck, that Italian time. The notebook page smoothed down, the pen poised over the page, always the risk: the first words written.

PURE GOLD CLASPS

IN A PLASTIC BAG UNDER THE SUGAR IN A WHITE CANISTER. In the pocket of a burgundy dress I used to wear to class. Toe of a snow boot. Wedged between the legs of the ironing board leaning against the wall in the laundry room, in the bottom of a shoebox full of fading photographs, in a pitcher of dried roses, under the drum in the toy chest, in a box of sanitary pads, under the cabbage and carrots in the fridge's vegetable bin.

Never slid between sheets or towels in the linen closet, nestled under the sweaters, nowhere near the mattress, or pillows, or bookcases, or handbags, or fake shaving cream, or tomato soup cans. Certainly not hollowed-out books.

WHEN THE CARABINIERI CAME, the chief said, "Choose a flowerpot in the garden and dig a hole under it." The tall, muscular one demonstrated, there, on top of a beam in the kitchen. "They can't look on top of all the beams in the house," he reasoned.

At two in the morning, we returned from a fine evening in Cortona. The Tuscan Sun Festival, in full frisson, had presented Jeremy Irons performing as Chopin; his wife, Sinéad Cusack, played George Sand, a vignette interspersed by music. Afterward, we'd dined at the postconcert party, applauding as the actors and musicians entered the courtyard of the museum. We lingered with friends over the lavish buffet and the local syrah poured by the winemaker. Yet another glorious evening under Tuscan stars.

We were at that time staying at our Little Red Riding Hood stone house in the chestnut forest. Our friend Alberto was our guest, and because we'd had an early small supper, then had left in a hurry for the concert, all the lights were left on in the house. His car was parked in the driveway.

Returning home late, we were planning to enjoy a last glass of something good outside in the balmy night air.

"Ed, did you leave the kitchen open?" I saw a rectangle of light falling on the herb garden outside the door.

"I did not!" he said, as we approached the wide-open door. Then we saw the alarm box on the hall floor.

"Don't go in," Alberto warned. "They may still be here." Ed called our friend who is head of the carabinieri, fifteen whole minutes away. He said they'd be here *subito*. I pictured Claudio climbing out of bed, muttering *dio mio*. Already, I was thinking of my jewelry.

The evening was calm and starry. When, after a few minutes, no sound emerged from the house, we entered. The back door was broken. Alberto's bag and iPad remained on the kitchen table. The front door was broken, glass everywhere. All the mirrors and paintings lay strewn on the floor. Our *ladri* had searched in vain for a wall safe. They'd flung drawers, books, sheets, and cushions—a chaos. The pristine

MacBook Air sat still on the desk, along with our two iPads. I stepped into the bedroom, anxious about whether they'd taken my jewelry. I admonished myself for not hiding it. I left everything in a pink cotton roll, a red satin Chinese pouch, and a zippered blue satin case. Usually, I tuck them behind folds of curtains on the floor, in the gift-wrapping drawer under a bundle of ribbons, in the dryer under a pile of T-shirts—so many ingenious places that I often forget where I've stashed them. Ed and my daughter always tease me about my places to hide my treasures. Once, one pouch was lost for six months, then found in Ed's toolbox in the garage.

I spotted a bracelet on the floor outside the mounds of up-turned clothes. Because the police had not arrived, I didn't want to touch anything. The white gold links on the brick gave me hope that I had not lost all the touching mementos Ed had given me throughout our marriage—the gold rope necklace with a sapphire clasp bought in Venice when he turned fifty. He'd said because of our happiness in all the years we'd shared. The romantic pearls with a strand of am-ethyst, and the subtle cascade of four-diamond earrings. I never had a lot of jewelry, only fifteen separate joys. But what I had was good. Really good. I wore one of them every day. No other objects I own have half the emotional meaning. There's something different about jewelry; it is deeply per-sonal in a way no other objects are.

The wrapped gift, a necklace, that I was waiting to give to my neighbor Chiara, who'd just had a baby, was untouched on a bench.

The carabinieri arrived and our friend the *mareschiallo*, the marshal, swept me into a huge hug. The three men in their spiffy uniforms looked like they could handle major crime. They combed the house. My invaded, ravished home. No use to look for fingerprints, they asserted, the thieves are not dumb, they wear gloves. They ascertained, as we already had from the way the glass scattered, that they entered by the upstairs stairway and exited downstairs. The mystery was, how did they get from upstairs to a not-obvious downstairs cabinet and rip out the alarm before thirty seconds elapsed? The only conclusion, a sad one for us, was that obviously the thieves knew where the alarm was located and made a beeline for it. We were left to think of all the workers over the years and which of them was a betrayer. The young guy who installed the shelves and whistled with the piercing sweetness of birdsong? The silent master plasterer? Someone we never would suspect?

We entered the bedroom, and I'm sure you've guessed: All the jewelry was gone. They had taken the time to untie the pink roll, unzip the blue satin pouch, remove the contents, and leave the holders in the pile of my underwear and the tumped-over drawers. The red pouch was gone. The one piece of costume jewelry, a string of glass beads, was rejected and remained in a corner of a drawer.

More hugs all around from the police, who were especially moved and kept repeating to one another that the pearls had come from my mother, a mother's jewelry being most resonant to them. Then erupted the discussion of future hiding places. A safe? Absolutely not. They maintained again that thieves are not stupid; they have tools to rip that wall safe right out and buzz into it. Should we have video surveillance? No, signore. You think they don't wear masks?

Not trusting banks—or wanting to hide income from tax authorities—Italians keep cash at home. Thieves are up on all the hiding places, but, as the tall, muscular policeman reasoned, they can't dig under all the flowerpots. I didn't say that every time I wanted my lapis earrings, I didn't want to unearth them from the garden. Besides, scorpions love living under pots. It was late. Anyway, I now had nothing to hide from any jewel thief. Let them break in and find a few spoons in coin silver. Ed and Alberto questioned the carabinieri about searching at gold dealers for the jewelry. Useless. The gold will be melted down by morning.

We were leaving for the USA in two days. We had the doors boarded, the alarm repaired. The rooms had to be put in order, the paintings rehung. Ed and I worked silently. We missed the last of the Tuscan Sun Festival. We were dealing with police reports and insurance. I'd never gotten around to insuring my jewelry beyond the household policy. (Beat on head again.) Everyone kept saying how awful the loss of such sentimental gifts, but by now I was thinking, yeah, and how awful the loss of all that gold at $2,000 an ounce. Could be anyone. As much as loss, the violation of a brutal break-in lingers. Your home invaded. You wear it like a heavy wet coat.

This precautionary tale has no silver—or gold—lining. Six weeks passed. Every time I got dressed I wished for my white gold necklace with the crystal box of happy diamonds that Ed gave me when one of my books became a bestseller, the pearl-and-gold link bracelet my daughter gave me, the weighty gold necklace with which I rewarded myself from a mean aunt's surprise inheritance, the amethyst earrings the color of Tuscan grapes in September, the old pearls that once broke in church and scattered while the choir sang "Jerusalem," the citrine sunburst necklace a new friend had given me that same day. Never worn.

"I know it's shallow," I said to my sister, "to be so upset over material things. I know it's a first, first world problem."

"Don't be silly," she answered. "You'll never get over this."

Not one of the great losses of the world, not important in the face of those struggling to survive, the stupid wars and terrorists, the fact that people do not respect the earth enough to take care of it, on and on. But, yes, the world is private, too, and when your home is ravaged and a lifetime's collection of intensely personal belongings is ripped away, a lingering sadness starts up. I felt stripped. Mentally assaulted. Really angry. I won't replace the jewelry, not even if I could. I'm sorry I won't be passing it on to my daughter and my nieces but so be it. Now that I know what it's like to lose it, I don't want to experience that again.

The thief's wife or girlfriend may at this moment have hidden inside a sock the handful of earrings, the bracelet, and the two pearl necklaces that couldn't be melted. Maybe her ugly husband yanked off the gold parts, but maybe he left them intact for her, love of his life, and in a few months she may lift out the creamy pearls and fasten the gold clasp around her neck. She may look in the mirror and try to imagine where they came from. She may lift her chin and straighten her shoulders. Maybe she will dare to wear the dangling lustrous pearl earrings. On that day, I may be at the market and see a woman lean over to buy apples, the pearls swinging out. Maybe not. Maybe they're sold in Russia.

I now own four pieces of valuable jewelry. Two I was wearing the night of the heist. One, my favorite gold bee necklace, I'd left downstairs in a kitchen drawer, meaning to take it upstairs later. Another bracelet was broken and piled in a dish in the dining room, waiting to be repaired. Where shall I hide them? Right now, they're in a small box in the bidet, with a hand towel flung casually over the bowl. No one ever would look in the bidet, would they?

When I returned to Italy after six weeks, a stranger had left at my house wooden salt and pepper grinders he made of several woods. He'd even left the coarse salt and the whole pepper to grind. Someone else left three soft hand-woven cotton dish towels, almost too nice to use. Friends to whom I'd lent the house left a well-selected case of Tuscan wines, a watercolor of the house, and kind notes. A woman from Poland sent a plaster angel. Our friend Gilda left lasagna and a roasted turkey breast stuffed with orange and chestnuts. All these spontaneous gifts leave me with nights to ponder their meaning—the loving spirit of what is given, the grand subtraction of what is taken away.

As the story circulated around town, everyone told me a story of their own losses or the losses of friends and family. Back in North Carolina, it was the same. Like labor sagas for the pregnant woman, these stories don't help; they only inspire further fear. But cumulatively, I had to see that I was not unique, at least, and for those who had life savings jammed in

a milk carton in the fridge, I was among the lucky, who'd
(only) lost "frivolous" jewelry.

Still. Jewelry isn't money. It's romance, heritage, an inner
concept of beauty. That's why those fragile earrings and delicate necklaces found in Etruscan tombs move us so with their
evocation of the ancient wearer. My daughter loves my mother's ring (her bluest of eyes, her generosity), and my mean
aunt's ring (who did she love, ever?) sparkles on her little fin-
ger. Hold tight, my darling. You don't want to lose them.

CUCINA POVERA /
THE POOR KITCHEN

DURING THE UGLY MONTHS-INTO-YEARS OF THE PANDEMIC, we were confined to our kitchens. Ingredients I took for granted, such as flour, yeast, whipping cream, and brown sugar, were erratically unavailable. Fear of shortages, fear of the unknown, spurred me to plant the largest vegetable garden of my life. As I weeded around the carrots and tied up tomatoes, I recalled my grandmother's stories of the Great Depression and English friends' memories of their parents' World War II rationing, then the intense deprivations long after. What came to mind vividly was my own admiration for *cucina povera*, the traditional cooking of the poor in Italy. In times of want, which historically have been all too frequent, a cook had to make do with what was available. Necessity becomes the brood mother of invention. The inconvenience of no whipping cream has nothing to do with the scrounging of the cook facing bare shelves.

Before I knew the term *cucina povera*, poor kitchen, I began to taste its inheritance. When Ed and I first visited the Tuscan trattorie in 1990, waiters offered two wines—*bianco* or *nero*—white or black. Menus adhered to tradition. This was fine with us—we loved wild boar with the wide pasta pappardelle, the hearty bean-and-bread soup *ribollita*, grilled sausages with fennel, and the hefty grilled *bistecca* with oil and rosemary. After a while, we began to seek out the one or two specialties of each trattoria: sharp marinated zucchini at one, raw artichoke salad and spinach gnocchi at another, the superb veal roast at a local hotel restaurant. One quality always stood out—the food was *genuino*. It tasted like what it was. The homemade wine, too. Some farmers were better vintners than others; I've had sour shellac at several tables. More often we quaffed down tumblers of earthy, fulsome "black" wine that tasted of the fruit it came from.

I noticed the difference between fresh pasta, often made with eggs, and the usual (also excellent) *asciuta*, dry pasta, made only from flour and water. (First clue: In earlier times, an egg might have been hard to come by.)

I'd brought several cookbooks along from the USA, but then I began to be invited into Tuscan homes, began to ask my neighbors how to make curly kale soup, or tortellini in *brodo* (start with a mature hen), or *pappa al pomodoro* (simplest of all tomato soups). I shelved the books. They seemed fussy. I woke up to the realization that the immense variety of Italian food was expressed fully—and spontaneously—by frugal home cooks using what they had, no matter how limited that might be. The authority was *nonna*, grandmother, or *bisnonna*, great-grandmother. None of my Italian friends used cookbooks at all—or even measuring cups and spoons, except sometimes for baking. And for that, most simply prepared crostata, fruit tarts, which they knew by heart. I've eaten at the best restaurants in New York and San Francisco, the ones with the hype, food shows, books. After dinners at the de Palme house and the Cardinali house and the Italiani house, I can't worship at those urban temples. Italian home cooks have a depth of information on seasonal ingredients, a vast range of dishes they serve, and an inborn aptitude for knowing what's ripe today. After years of cooking with them, I'm still in awe of the impromptu genius of the traditional cook. Follow the dropped crumbs and you're led back to *cucina povera.*

AT THE COURTS OF the dukes, cardinals, and royalty, they had the freshest vegetables, best oil, cream, the choice cuts of meat. Aristocratic banquets featured stuffed peacocks with the tail in full spread, spun-sugar bird cages, succulent roasts, and fanciful desserts. That tradition was not handed down. These were: *lampredotto* (the cow's fourth stomach), tripe, stuffed pigs' feet, and sausages. The *quinto quarto,* the fifth quarter, meaning offal, and discarded knuckles, tails, feet, and neck were left to the workers.

Cuisine was either high or low because for much of history, Italy had a small middle class, unlike France, which developed a restaurant culture and an elaborate bourgeois cuisine. This is why, by my lights, Italians appreciate everything. Parts of the pig and cow I never thought would see light are served forth with relish, along with, hard to behold, a platter of songbirds. Hold one by the beak and bite, cracking bones and all. I surreptitiously have slipped many morsels of lamb heart, intestines of unweaned veal, and rabbit kidney to the side. My friends love this country food. At the home of Antonello, our electrician, who has big casual dinners, we saw five boys head back to the stove for second bowlfuls of snails simmered in tomatoes and broth.

When I widen the aperture, I see *cucina povera* as a way of thinking and being, as well as of cooking. I'm always looking for what shapes the people of a particular spot on Earth: How does the land, history, and climate act to form the people into who they are? What does the poor kitchen have to do with character, with culture, even with how we are living on the planet? What does it have to do with my kitchen today?

Cameramen from Rome, delivery drivers, journalists from Milan, chance travelers from the Veneto or Sicily, who come to my house in Tuscany may be citified but within minutes they're asking about the olives, testing the plums, pocketing a few lemons to take home. My neighbors are out for daily walks but they're not just walking. They're picking dandelions, spiky greens, snapping my fennel flowers! Jump a ditch and risk a broken collarbone for a few sprigs of asparagus. A foraging instinct spirals in the DNA. Foraging is kind of in with chefs worldwide, but I'm not thinking of a morning out collecting seaweed or fiddlehead ferns. Italians forage out of an abiding bond with seasons and land.

Those genius cooks of *cucina povera*, what did they look for? And now, too?

In spring, after the gathering of yarn-thin wild asparagus, we move toward the time for crunchy green almonds, picked before the nut develops. In Puglia, *lampascioni*, wild hyacinth bulbs, are a treat. In early summer, pick young stinging nettles and borage for filling ravioli. Fig trees pop up all over Italy, even in the pavement cracks of parking lots. Get up before dawn to gather snails from damp stone walls. Green walnuts for making *nocino*, a spicy after-dinner drink. Truffles and mushrooms, of course. Fennel, for the pollen, flowers, and seeds. What a treat to find sour cherries. *Mentuccia*, wild mint, to flavor meats and in the south of Italy to wrap with ferns around cheeses. Chestnuts! In hard times, chestnuts were lifesavers, gathered for making flour as well as for roasting, stuffing, and serving after steeping them in a little wine. The difficult taste to acquire is the revered dessert *castagnaccio*, like a thick crêpe—a poor kitchen sweet if ever there was one. Chestnut flour, a bit of olive oil, a little rosemary. No sugar. Even with latter-day additions of raisins and pine nuts, it's still flat and ugly—loved for tastes-like-home reasons.

Foraging—the opposite of selecting produce coated with wax, plastered with stickers, or strawberries from Chile in winter. No prewashed lettuce compares with raunchy *puntarella*, a green related to chicory. Slice the stalks and soak them in salted cold water. The pieces curl and add punch to any salad. During the rush of summer bounty, cooks preserve as their mothers before them the extra artichokes, peppers, beans, eggplants, cucumbers. *Sott'olio*, under oil, or pickled, they're ready to be pulled out when needed. Domenica and Gilda, great impresarios of their family kitchens, each put up around three hundred jars of tomatoes at the end of summer. Fennel flowers and tomatoes dry on screens in the sun. The porcini and chestnut gathering among the majestic golden trees in fall signals the beginning of dinners by the fire. This is true today, true when I first arrived, and true as far back as memory goes.

Cucina povera's defining heritage—Italians have a deep-rooted connection to the soil. A second gift: a waste-not philosophy—crucial for us Earth dwellers. I'd noticed on trash day, tiny bags were set out for pickup, while mine loomed embarrassingly large. We've focused on recycling but neglected the sheer waste that accumulates daily.

Cucina povera: Use every ounce of the pig, snout to tail, grill whatever your fishing line pulls in, grow what you can, shop frequently so that bunch of carrots or broccoli doesn't wilt before you get to it. The habit arose from lack of refrigeration but results in less waste. Shopping daily seems not a chore but a time to hear the news and talk about what you're going to do with the kumquats, beets, or cardoons.

Imitating friends who learned at home from their mothers, I chop the stems of parsley and arugula. They're as good as chives. Peel the rough broccoli stems, slice and steam. Use celery and radish leaves, carrot and fennel greens in salads and for garnish. Bitter greens grace the ear-shaped pasta orec-chiette. Nonna would use all this. She'd add the rind of Parmigiano to her soup for flavor, too. The primary waste-not example is bread. Loaves are bought almost daily from the local *forno.* This habit goes way back. (Oddly, the word connects with "fornication"—prostitutes used to gather around the bread ovens for warmth.)

There's going to be leftover bread. *Ecco,* the summery bread salad, *panzanella. Ecco,* the stuffed baked vegetables, *ribollita,* and bruschette, vehicle for a thousand toppings. A local man who was a child during World War II told me his breakfast then was a slice of bread moistened with wine and sugar. Babies are given a hunk to sooth their gums.

Before a loaf turns hard as a baseball bat, there are the blessed crumbs. Who could imagine the myriad uses of humble bread crumbs? Toasted and tossed over pasta, crumbs in the poor kitchen mimicked Parmigiano. Add an anchovy if you have one, with a splash of olive oil. Or sauté big crumbs with herbs and red pepper flakes. Almost out of flour? Mix some with bread crumbs for a semblance of pasta. Now I never toss out bread. Crumbs top soups, baked pastas, or salads. I love the story of the *arsa* flour in Puglia, which is valued for the great round loaves of that region—some weighing eight, ten pounds—bread that is so hearty and delicious, you find yourself eating it like cake. Landowners used to burn off the wheat fields after harvest and the workers culled the ground, collecting charred grains to supplement their stash of flour. The toasty flavor became desired, and now you can enjoy the magnificent bread made from *farina arsa*, toasty wheat flour, in the many great *fornos* of that region, especially in Altamura and Orsara.

Driving around Italy, you spot the old home-place planting configuration of a wheat field bordered by olive trees and grape vines. There you have it, the sacred trinity: wheat, oil, wine. *Cucina povera*'s triumph: wheat, which means pasta and bread. And what the home cooks did with pasta! Hundreds of shapes, whimsical, practical ridges to hold the sauce, delicate plump pillows, nails, radiators, braids, spirals, stars, elbows, lilies, half-sleeves, butterflies. Poetry and fun, and, most of all, inventiveness from flour and water—nothing more basic and yet even the simplest accompaniment can reach the sublime. Chickpeas or bitter greens, any bitter green crushed into a pesto, a handful of herbs, whatever you have. Good oil, and, with luck, a few shavings of truffle. Pasta's infinite varieties prove the brilliance and solace of the poor kitchen.

The transformative ingredient in Italian food remains great olive oil. We began pressing ours as soon as we cleared the land that had been abandoned for thirty years, and later launched an olive oil business. Picking olives in October connected us with the ancient wheel of the seasons. Olive oil, in the Mediterranean world, is not just an ingredient, it's a libation, a holy substance that connects your home to the earth and promotes a sense of belonging in time.

Our brand-new oil, glowing like liquid emeralds, was a revelation. Trying to duplicate my friend Giusi's stuffed zucchini, her *arista*, pork roast, even her plain green beans, we'd fallen short. Ours were good. Not as good. We watched closely. Whereas we drizzled olive oil into the pan, she flipped off the spout and poured. She used three times what we did. Four times. Discussing this with the owner of the hardware store, she said flatly, "Our oil will not make you fat."

We believed her. We copied. Our food sparkled. Douse your salads and grilled steak—but also rub a daub on an insect bite, baby's umbilical cord, or stretch marks, or dry skin. Steep some with lavender and flavor your bathwater. Pour a dribble on an orange and sprinkle with salt. Fry with it, yes, regardless of what you read to the contrary. For her family of four, Gilda uses one pound of butter per year. But she uses, as we do, at least a liter of olive oil a week.

We'd had things backward. While we meted out the olive oil in our California kitchen, we always poured the wine freely. After a dinner for eight, we'd haul about that many bottles out to the bin. Among our Italian friends, we noticed that after a party there would be only three or four empty wine bottles, and equally that many water bottles. The Italians drank as much water as wine. (Fortunately, the custom of adding water to wine has faded.) And the wine drinking commences only when the food is served. Only a few friends thought to offer wine before dinner. We got it! The pairing of wine with food forms a part of the balancing act that comprises the Italian meal.

Why do Italians seem to feel at home in their lives? The abiding connection to nature and respect for what it gives. We become happy when we fall into natural rhythms, seasons, expectations. I love to see the *ritmo,* the rhythm, of dinner, which arrives in four distinct courses. Antipasto, primo, secondo, dolce. Each is savored and concentrated on. At the call *"A tavola!"* to the table, you flush with pleasure; you are coming into a celebratory ambiance. Something wonderful is about to happen. No one speculates on how many calories are hiding in the ravioli. I used to think the word *sinful* was the automatic adjective for *dessert*. Even in Sicily, where they really know about hard-core desserts, it's a concept I've never heard. Nor have I heard of a dish referred to as "your protein" or "a carb," and there's no dreary talk at the table about glutens or fat content. After a long Italian dinner, I feel not only the gift of exceptional company, food, and wine but also an inexplicable sense of well-being, of revival. This healthy appreciation is directly connected to *cucina povera*. Revere what you have. Food is natural, eaten with moderation, yes, but with gusto. Here we are at the heart of the matter. Those great-grandmothers knew all about gratitude and respect for what's served forth.

"You never grow old at the table," Tuscans say. The grinding wheel of time stops at the dining room door, leaving those who pass the pasta bowl suspended in the aromas of rising steam. In my years in rural Italy, growing vegetables, cooking, and foraging, everything I knew about wine and food enlarged. It's transforming when you feel doors you didn't know were closed swing open.

The wartime, hard-times grandmothers facing meager cupboards developed the most loved cuisine in the world. Their heritage could not be more *genuino*. Here's the poet Cesare Pavese: "A gulp of my drink," he wrote, "and my body can taste the life / of plants and of rivers." The abundant ancestral table remains set for the best life has to offer.

Household Shrine

"Do you believe in God?" I ask my neighbor. He answers, "No, but I believe in Mary."

Mary, who intercedes, who sallies forth with our prayers, who watches over, who suffered as all mothers suffer and more, who calms, who comforts—it's she who appears in the household shrine called a Madonnina. She's a friend, divine, but still a friend. We think of her when we wear blue and when the rosemary blooms. If God appeared on Earth, we might hide our eyes in fear, but Mary, we would invite Mary to sit at our table.

She seems, too, to be the most sited among the holy: At Fatima in Portugal, Lourdes, Guadalupe, the Black Madonna in Czestochowa, Poland—so many manifestations of her presence. We travel to those miraculous places hoping to breathe the air she breathed, to brush the caper bush where her skirts passed, hoping for miracles.

Near Ephesus stands the last home of the Virgin Mary. Certainly fantasy, the legend of the site represents a wish of ours that her last home be located. A German mystic published a book in 1841 describing her vision of Maria at Ephesus, and archaeologists later found a fourth-century ruin and grave there. That the fourth century is many, many years after Mary's time has not deterred visitors ever since. When I visited, heaving busloads emptied into the parking lot and headed to the little stone house. These pilgrims, appealing for her intercession or giving thanks for the same, have attached to a wall whatever was at hand, handkerchiefs, Kleenex, pantyhose, small photos, and pieces of maps.

Another home of Maria, her birthplace in Nazareth, was transported by heavenly assistance in 1291 to Trsat in Croatia, then again was lifted in a great angelic puff in 1294 and flown to Loreta, near Ancona, where it still can be visited. Clearly, the connection of Mary and the significance of the house have deep mythic juju. The Madonna and the longing for home are seamless. And so in Italy she naturally becomes the one to station near the door or in the piazza or at a crossroads along the road to home. In a purely secular sense, her shrines punctuate the landscape. Like cypress trees, like bell towers, like stone walls and olive terraces, shrines add their particular character and depth. Imagine Italy without them.

Miracles prompt long pilgrimages, but the Maria of the household shrines is for everyday life. *Protect this house,* I saw scrawled on a little card propped in a shrine on Capri. In private chapels, little family churches, roadside shrines, and bedroom altars, sometimes you find Jesus on the cross, or sometimes Saint Francis, but the image of the Madonna is ubiquitous. In Cortona, beneath a neon-ringed Madonna and the statue of Santa Margherita with her attribute, a devoted dog, a small real dog often sleeps. In the doctor's office, there's Maria plastered over the hand towel dispenser. The gas station, the carabinieri office, the butcher's shop, the bank, the blacksmith's, the mechanic's garage—look up and there she is, often with a twig of olive branch behind her image, and often next to the nudie calendar. She has ubiquity and higher power. Even nonbelievers acknowledge her reach. "There is no God and Mary is his mother" is attributed to the philosopher Santayana. She's in the air, everywhere, down to earth. She has a stare that nearly burns through the metal grate she's often behind. She's not bothered by roses gone off, pigeons pausing in flight, or sun angling into her eyes. Do her eyes follow as we pass? If I reach to touch a foot or hem of robe, will I feel a small shock? Is a kitschy Madonna still powerful? Did the artist love the chalky blue? Did he sleep the sleep of the blessed after painting this?

One early summer morning in Naples, I wandered around visiting Madonna shrines. I didn't follow a guidebook, didn't think where I was going. (This probably was not a good way to get to know the city.) My only goal was to pay attention because the shrine with the image of the Madonna is everywhere—it's difficult to concentrate after you've seen five. Although some shrines announce themselves on the corners of important streets, most are more unobtrusive, demure, unostentatious. If they're at human level, their ledges for flowers are stuffed with plastic hydrangeas and real potted azaleas and cut gladioli. One of my favorites housed a tomato can full of garden roses. Others have softly winking electric bulbs over them, or a humming rim of neon blue. Some are covered in hardened rivulets of candle wax. A few are abandoned and you wonder why when others nearby are not. They are folk art. They are sacred. They occur at the junctures of spirituality, the impulse to create art, and the concern for everyday life. They are above all made by someone's hand, some uncle or stonemason friend. Maybe he chooses the form and materials—brick vs. stone—then a discussion one night over pasta settled the matter: Lucia would buy the statue, Cecilia would mix the right paint color, and she and Mama would paint the inside of the niche marine blue, then Don Antonio would come to consecrate it. Most saints stand under an arc of brick or stone or painted plaster. An arc is a part of a circle that represents the apparent course of a heavenly body, sun or moon, Venus or Mars, suggesting the same scope for Mary, saint, or archangel.

Finished, the shrine becomes a focal point that wasn't there before, a piece of architecture, yes, but not like a new door or window that wouldn't cause anyone to notice. The new shrine stands out, a hot spot in the landscape. It becomes meaningful not only to the family that constructed it, but to those who pass, including me on a June morning, peering at the curled notes and saints' cards laid among the flowers, and the metal cut-out arms and legs that someone running on an image and a prayer hoped would bring a cure to an injured limb. Does Maria read thoroughly the minds of those passing, those who ignore her, as if she were a lamppost, a mailbox, a hotel sign? And the minds of those who stop, whether they're longing for a way out of their world, or thankful that they found a way into it? What's absent may be as mysterious as what you see: The shadows and gestures of those walking by, those who have passed the shrine so many times that it has become a mirror into which they can no longer see their reflections.

At our house, we have a stone niche at the entrance to the driveway. Inside there is a Della Robbia–style Madonna and Bambino. At the first moment I saw it, I also saw Bramasole and knew instinctively that this would be home. During the early years, while we were clearing the abandoned land of brambles, a very solitary man used to bring flowers to the shrine every day. He wore his coat over his shoulders, even in the blast furnace heat of August, and he paid no attention to us wielding clippers and weed whackers on the terraces above. On his daily mission, he took the flowers from the day before, dropped them in the ditch, swept out the shrine with the side of his hand, and propped up his new bouquet of yarrow or dog roses or poppies.

After years of his visits, suddenly they stopped. No one in town seemed to know this man. He never returned and I assume he died. Our neighbor's ancient mother, too, used to visit the shrine daily. She brought her own offerings of flowers until she died. I also began to keep a jar of roses or a handful of daffodils from the garden in the shrine. Just as the two visitors died, an odd twist of fate occurred. Readers of my books about Tuscany began to visit the house. They started to leave mementos in the shrine—coins, pinecones, wildflowers, candles, pretty rocks, notes. Even bottles of wine from Hungary and Poland. Groups photograph one another in front of the shrine. Our neighbor Placido rides by on his horse and bows his head and crosses himself, In the name of the Father and the Son and the Holy Ghost. Katia comes jogging by, arms pumping a sign of the cross. Chiara, our neighbors' daughter, has taken over her grandmother's vigil: When we return after a long absence, we are certain to be welcomed home by Mary, a lighted votive, and a vase of whatever blooms from Chiara's garden.

THE ROMANS HAD THEIR household, as well as public shrines, for their many gods. At home, at least three were honored: Lar, the god of houses; Janus, looking in and out of the doorway; and Vesta, goddess of the hearth. Lares, tutelary deities, or ancestors watched over the house, as did penates, other gods of the house, who focused on the family's food and cupboards. The shrines we find today are late expressions of ancient tradition. They still enliven the lost roads, the corners of villages, and the gated entrances to towns. I have seen impromptu shrines on the dashboards of battered Fiats. They are not only for prayer or to pay respect. The shrine comes from a human need to anchor the foundation of the casa, strada, or città to something divine. Walking around Naples, I discovered the explanation for my own fascination. A piece of intense attention paid is also a fragment of the divine. The true image hands back a truth.

A shrine, unlike a *santuario,* a sanctuary, isn't usually a destination point but more of an object one sees on the way to your neighbor's house, the grocery store, the park. What a pause at a shrine brings to this moment of daily life is stasis, in the Greek sense of "a state of standing." Linger a moment. What are you feeling? There's at least a moment in the hurry to do this and that, a recognition that the Virgin Mary (or occasionally an Annunciation angel) is a still point, fixed forever, while you, temporal and fragile, move on, return, move on. We're magnetically drawn to Mary's roadside homes— the brave and scared, the complacent and adventurous, the free and chained, and the curious. The shrines have force, pulling to them those who need to be pulled.

EXILE 2020

THIS MORNING, MY SIXTH DAY OF "SHELTERING AT HOME,"
I thought of John Keats quarantined in the Bay of Naples.
Unlike unwilling literary exiles such as Dante and Ovid, ban-
ished for political reasons, Keats chose to leave his home in
damp and rainy England, seeking the sun of Italy for his
health.

In October 1820, typhus raged in Naples. With his artist
friend Joseph Severn, Keats rocked in the harbor for ten days,
not nearly the *quaranta giorni,* forty days that give us our
word *quarantine.* Before this journey, Keats always felt intense
melancholy. He wrote, ". . . mortality / Weighs heavily on
me like unwilling sleep" ("On Seeing the Elgin Marbles for
the First Time"). And in the smooth pentameter of "Ode to a
Nightingale": "I have been half in love with easeful Death."
Not a holiday, this voyage out of England was a desperate
trip. His cough had grown steadily worse. Since the morning
he'd seen a splotch of blood on his pillow, he knew he had
little chance of surviving the consumption that had invaded
his lungs. His last ditch: Go to Rome. Meanwhile, exile at sea.

I have seen Naples from his vantage of a ship anchored
offshore. One of the most sublime locations in the world, that

sweep of coast stacked with apricot, carmine, azure, and rose villas, the blue, blue U of the harbor, the emphatic outline of Vesuvius anchoring the view. See Naples and die, the saying goes. I'm a bit stir crazy in under a week; ten days of enforced idleness could seem like a year. (Not one on the cruise ships recently stuck offshore reports having a fine time.)

Keats had a not-at-all-poetic upbringing, with almost everyone he loved dying throughout his childhood. He suffered instability, poverty, and constant fights with bullies who teased him for his "lack of inches." After this tough and tragic early youth, he apprenticed at fourteen to a doctor for medical training, a hideous experience, followed by other gruesome years training at a hospital. Along the way, he fell in love with poetry and spent all his spare time studying and writing. Abandoning medicine, he clawed his way into a literary life and only wanted his name to be "among the English poets." That it is.

His brief period of quarantine fascinates me. Keats, almost twenty-five, with only four more months to live, already had felt himself "insubstantial, as though My whole existence is already posthumous." He had no way to know that to far-distant readers like me, his life story would be triumphant. The sad epitaph on his gravestone in the cemetery in Rome says, *Here lies one whose name was writ in water.* How wrong.

A quarantine letter survived, to Mrs. Brawn, the mother of Fanny, the young woman he loved and would never see again. "O what an account I could give you of the Bay of Naples if I could once more feel myself a Citizen of this world," he wrote, and "Give my love to Fanny and tell her, if I were well there is enough in this Port of Naples to fill a quire of Paper—but it looks like a dream."

A quire of paper. That's four large sheets of parchment folded to create twenty-four pages. Imagine that he had covered them with descriptions of the so-near-so-far city on the shimmering water. Italy. A moon wobbling up, casting silver glints on the domes, the far-off bells resonating out to sea, warm humid air to breathe deeply. I see him leaning on the rail. All *half in love with easeful death* thoughts forgotten. In quarantine, he faced a full stop. He found a raging desire to live. He left behind the young man full of verve and romanticism, who courted melancholy in his poems. Now here's this bright, sublime bay and everything pulls him toward life, home, love. But life becomes a dream vision across the waters. And no energy for scrawling across a quire of paper.

In a letter written shortly after he disembarked from the *Maria Crowther,* his panic strikes out like a bird caught inside a room. He cannot imagine he won't see Fanny again. "I am afraid to write to her—to receive a letter from her—to see her handwriting would break my heart—even to hear of her anyhow, to see her name written would be more than I can bear."

Across two hundred years, the anguish still vibrates. If he'd recovered, if he'd been able to go home to Fanny, able to wander Italy instead of looking out the window onto the Spanish Steps, so far from Hampstead Heath, I wonder if his poetry would have changed.

This sixth day, grounded, I spent at home with Keats. "Much have I travell'd in the realms of gold," he wrote. Me, too. In college I thought that "gold" meant dreams, but I found out the gold referred to the gilt on the sides of treasured books. My Keats volumes aren't gold-bound, they're yellowed and embarrassingly underlined, especially "The Eve of St. Agnes." I recall first reading it and finding a breakthrough realization about writing. There's the margin note I wrote in lavender ink: *color, touch, smell, taste—activate two sensory links and your line is irresistible*. Knowing his "A thing of beauty is a joy forever" remains a touchstone.

My cat crawls on the sofa and I try out various immortal lines on him, but he stares out the window, not caring that we're in the grip of an epic virus that is swooping around the world, a biblical swarm, lighting capriciously where it will, like the bacillus that landed in, latched onto, and bloomed in the poet's lungs. We don't know if we're inside for ten days or the full *quarantina*. Or longer. Full stop. Will Vesuvius blow? We don't know much.

Which brings me back to Keats. He aspired to what he called Negative Capability, when one is "capable of being in uncertainties, Mysteries, doubts, without any irritable reaching after fact and reason." At the end of this quarantined day, that's my takeaway. No need for *irritable reaching*. Facts and reasons can change. *Capable*, a strong word. *Being*, an active presence. *Uncertainty*, a liquid state in which you float, dream, and take in the view.

III

SOUTHERN EXPOSURE

HOME IS WHERE ONE STARTS FROM.

—*T. S. Eliot*

CROSS CREEK BELONGS TO THE WIND AND
THE RAIN, TO THE SUN AND THE SEASONS,
TO THE COSMIC SECRECY OF SEED,
AND BEYOND ALL, TO TIME.

—*Marjorie Kinnan Rawlings*

IF ADVENTURES WILL NOT BEFALL
A YOUNG LADY IN HER OWN VILLAGE,
SHE MUST SEEK THEM ABROAD.

—*Jane Austen*

THE HOUSE ON
SOUTH LEE STREET

~→⊹⊱

PLACE IS FATE. I ALWAYS HAVE KNOWN THAT. I WAS DRIVING across the Golden Gate Bridge to my California home when my sister called from Atlanta. "DJ the DJ's house is for sale— want to make a big offer?" Behind his back, we called our grandfather John Henry Mayes (aka Daddy Jack) DJ the DJ. Proud and bossy, he was as far from a DJ as one could get.

The ancient taproot sense of home suddenly twined through the phone and down my spine. Her friend Dynamite, from our south Georgia hometown, had called her. (In our town people keep holdover nicknames such as hers, which comes from the time this lovely matron was just dynamite as she pranced down the football field as the drum majorette.)

"Dynamite says it's elegant. A beautiful restoration. That I should buy the old place, come home, and be among my people again," my sister says. I hear the edge of sarcasm in her voice.

"What did you tell her?"

Laughter. "I said that was the last house in the United States I'd want to buy."

The House, as our family called it, symbolized home. My father, Garbert, grew up there. He was called Boofa. When he was a baby, his sister Hazel could not say "beautiful." It remains a prime source of my lifelong obsession with homes, interiors, and gardens. Built in 1906, by the mid-century The House already seemed venerable with its wraparound porch, a massive magnolia out front, six fireplaces, and a graceful curving staircase. I loved the wide upstairs hall lined with chests full of scrapbooks, and brownish photographs, my aunt Hazel's layers of rose and cream taffeta, blue silk, and burgundy velvet ball gowns carefully preserved in tissue for decades after the last bars of "The Darktown Strutter's Ball" ended. The Big Ben chimes of the clock in the foyer marked time in the big silence of nights when I slept over. The secret bell under my grandmother's foot at the head of the table summoned Fanny Brown with her platters of peppery smothered quail. The scent of the house—cigar smoke, Shalimar, damp ashes, fried food—has hit me in various unlikely faraway places and catapulted me again through the back screen door into the celery-green kitchen. A mirrored sphere on a pedestal in the yard showed my two-year-old cheeks distorted by the convex ball. Move aside and see silvery face-size hydrangeas and the huge oak tree shimmer. In my novel *Swan,* I tried to re-create the same sense I felt as a child in my grandparents' house on South Lee Street, a feeling akin to watching animated gold dust in a shaft of sunlight.

When I was eleven, for the entirety of a summer vacation at Sea Island I played over and over a record of Stephen Vincent Benét's "John Brown's Body," memorizing "for wherever the winds of Georgia run, / It smells of peaches long in the sun." This I believed, although the winds in those parts usually carried only the noxious odor of the paper mills in

Brunswick. His sense of the beauty of the landscape mesmer-ized me. I loved, too, Sidney Lanier's "The Marshes of Glynn" and drove my family crazy in the car as I shouted out "As the marsh-hen secretly builds on the watery sod / Behold I will build me a nest on the greatness of God / . . . Oh, like to the greatness of God is the greatness within / The range of the marshes, the liberal marshes of Glynn."

In high school, I began to read Flannery O'Connor from over in Milledgeville, Carson McCullers from Columbus, Con-rad Aiken, born in Savannah, and the farther-flung Thomas Wolfe, James Agee, Eudora Welty, and, of course, the legend-ary William Faulkner. In the warp and weft of their books, I found a correspondence to a perception I felt of the intertwin-ing of place and character. I knew the force of the southern landscape, its violent hurricanes and tornadoes, the sun that can scorch your soul, even the uncertain nature of the land itself, where small islands bearing trees float in the swamps, where quicksand could grab your dog, and where the land itself might just drop from under your feet when limestone gave way, creat-ing sinkholes that surged with green water.

And that breeze smelling of peaches? Even better were the rooms scented with magnolia blossoms, which filled the fire-places more often than fire. I loved the sculptural beauty of dogwood choreographing the air and the massive pink aza-leas mounded against screened porches. Rising crop dust from plowed and DDT-sprayed fields gave us splendid, smeared popsicle-colored sunsets. On Sunday afternoons when we "rode around," I always made my parents stop the car so I could wade in clear-running creeks or look over the sides of wooden bridges sinking into black water with ghoulish cypress knees growing out of it. I remember reading *The Mind of the South,* and agreeing with W. J. Cash that the southerner takes the romantic view of the world because of the blue air around moss-hung trees. We don't see reality, he thought, instead we see a softer world.

Literature gave voice to my groping, instinctive ideas. I've kept that knowledge even though I've lived all over the map. In Tuscany, I learned again that a powerful landscape never can be just a backdrop because it's working on you, sculpting you into a shape of its own.

When I bought Bramasole, situated under an Etruscan wall and a Medici fortress, I knew that the house already was at home on that hillside. The layers of time were as visible as the layers of ocher, sienna, and rose paint on the crumbling stucco facade. The road below the house is named Strada della Memoria, Street of Memory, for the cypresses planted for the war dead. The view includes a distant golden villa, built in the eighteenth century for the visit of a pope. He stayed one night. From my place, the villa acts as a still point in the landscape. I can tell time by where the sun hits the facade. Sense of place? I thought that living in my house would be my way into a life in Italy, and that turned out to be right.

THE HOUSE ON LEE Street partially burned when I was in college. My grandmother Frances was long dead. My grandfather fled the flames in the night and died of shock two days later. Aunt Hazel had the exterior of the house restored, replacing the gracious wraparound porch with too-thin columns. For all my adult life and until Hazel died, the shell of the house was maintained on the outside, down to the polished brass knocker and marigolds along the sidewalk. "Tacky," my mother said. "Marigolds have nothing to do with anything."

Hazel, on her pilgrimages to the past, rode by and murmured, "Doesn't the house look good? I announced my engagement to Wilford to all twelve of my beaux, who sat around me on those steps." Eye roll from my mother, smirk from me at the word *beaux*. Meanwhile, Hazel lived in a tropical tiled house in Miami, which she said, always with an explosion of tears, would never be home. She had *hiraeth*, a Welsh word meaning the feeling for a home that can't ever be revisited or never really existed. Her Spanish Mediterranean home was a thousand times more interesting than her parents' late Victorian, but the square white house on the corner of Lee and Lemon had captured her heart, and she never let go.

Here's the crazy part, the haunting part, the unforgettable part, the part that made my sister say, "It's the last house in the United States I'd want to buy"—inside, the house was still burned. The baby grand, charred, leaned under the sagging staircase; the walls were black, and the furniture sticks of glassy ash. I did not write about this in my southern novel *Swan*. The metaphors felt too dense to sort out. I wonder how many small children peered in those windows and ran for their lives.

One college professor of mine claimed that the southern sense of place derives from the lost war. He meant, of course, the War Between the States, as it was then called. "We are the only people in America to fight for our land and have our land scoured," he proclaimed. "We have a sense of loss that never will be overcome." I did not believe him. I felt too shaped by the land itself, not some far-off war. I came to the study of history with a conviction that wars are given far too much space in the texts. I wanted an explanation that came from hidden wells, water hyacinths, moonshine, hunting rifles, hat-boxes, walking rain, cottonmouths, sheet lightning, scare-crows, lynchings, canopied beds, sinkholes, cotton bolls, auctioned humans, palmettos, ether vials, moonvine, and screen doors slamming on a summer morning. A place's icons are what move inside us, compel us toward what we are becoming.

Living in Tuscany reiterated this primary knowledge. My house became my icon. As it moved into my psyche, it seemed timeless. The House—my oldest playtime, my six-windowed childhood room a location for dreaming, the hideouts for everyday or sublime creativity and a chance to be myself in another version. Home, a deep-water mooring where you rise and fall. All old houses are full of invisible spirits, benevolent or otherwise. Whatever memories abide, they seep through the floors, and into your life. At Bramasole, something real imparts as soon as I return. I feel surges of happiness. I feel profoundly settled at home.

SOMEONE BOUGHT MOTHER MAYES and Daddy Jack's house. I can imagine heart-pine floors brought from another ruin, blue silk at the long windows, the latticed back porch where someone solemn might sit shelling lady peas. Attention lav-ished on every threshold and windowpane, changing the house's fate. The owners perhaps will not know everything of its burned history, but the disappearing ink of the past always will become visible. The little girl moving her dollhouse into Garbert's old room may, fifty years hence, imagine someone dancing in claret velvet, may prefer hydrangeas to all flowers, or may wake from a panic dream of fire rapidly consuming a curving staircase.

The Monumental Cakes of Frankye Davis Mayes

"Lord in heaven," my father said, as my mother entered the dining room with her coconut cake aloft. She gently lowered it onto the table. Fluffy and white, cosseted in coconut, the huge cake was too big to fit any plate we had, so it was iced on a piece of cardboard covered in foil, with white paper doilies fitted around the bottom, as though the cake sat on snowflakes. In early spring, she ringed the base with pink camellias; in summer, a wreath of orange and yellow nasturtiums; and during the winter holidays, tiny pinecones spray-painted gold, probably toxic.

My job in the preparation was to sit in the driveway with four coconuts, a bowl, an ice pick, and a hammer. I smacked the icepick into the eye of the coconut, drained out the liquid, then smashed open the shell. Getting the "meat" out wasn't easy, and then the brown rind must be picked away and the hunks shredded. I didn't like to cook but I liked to watch my mother cream the cup of butter with three cups of sugar, separating the entire carton of twelve eggs, and beating the whites into the butter and sugar. She saved the yolks in a bowl that she covered with a plastic, elasticized thing like a miniature shower cap. She then stirred into the batter a cup of milk, a splash of vanilla, and then—gradually—five cups of flour that she'd sifted with two teaspoons of baking powder. Sometimes she baked the cake in three round pans, but usually she liked two oblong pans because of the nice square slices from a rectangular cake.

The glory is the icing. All that fresh coconut! She cooked four cups of sugar and a cup of water to what she called "a long thread." When it cooled a bit, she folded in four stiffly beaten egg whites. Biting her lip, she beat hard until the icing turned glossy. Then she stirred in almost all the coconut and spread the first layer all over with the smooth frosting. After she finished the top layer, she sprinkled on the rest of the coconut. One hundred calories a bite? We didn't think of calories, ever.

Resplendent on the dining room table, the cake seemed more than just a cake. It was the cake of cakes. Or so we thought, until my mother brought forth, in a week or so, the next regal edifice, her lemon cheesecake, my father's favorite. It was not a cheesecake as we know them: the tangy lemon curd filling must have reminded someone of curdy cheese. Looking at the recipe, I see a plain cake magically transformed by the divine, creamy filling and finished with Great-Aunt Besta's white icing. I have no talent with tricky white icing. No matter whose recipe I use, the ingredients refuse to fluff. In fact, I suffer from Fear of White Icing. But my mother had the gift of frothy, glistening icings. Among her recipes, I find three, each of which I quickly could reduce to a limp glob.

The citrus filling is simple. She melted a half a stick of butter in a small saucepan, added the grated rind and juice of two plump lemons, added three beaten eggs, a tiny pinch of salt, and three quarters of a cup of sugar. She cooked it on a medium burner until, as the recipe instructs, it "falls in flakes."

That is the only instruction on the yellowed paper, and that's true of all her recipes. I suppose she didn't bother to write procedures that she knew how to do. She might note, "cook to syrup," or "mix and BEAT," "soft ball stage," or "hard crack." Without such sure instincts, I've floundered when I've tried some of her recipes—one leaden lane cake into the trash—but I can perfectly re-create my favorite of her repertoire, the splendid, rich caramel cake, as monumental as my sister seemed in her wedding dress. I've served this every Thanksgiving of my grown-up life. This grandiose caramel cake (and please say "cara-mell" because that middle "a" gives the word its silky richness) contains, with filling and frosting, eight cups of sugar. That's why I limit it to Thanksgiving, when everything is over the top anyway. The toil is long; the results are sublime. Everyone wants to fall on the floor in a swoon, that is, except for when I served it in Italy to friends who pushed it around on their plates, all finally admitting, *troppo zucchero,* too much sugar! I don't know—maybe you must have been spoon-fed, maybe it's one of those things like *castagnaccio,* the flat and bitter chestnut cake that I push around on my plate in Italy. For them it was a childhood treat and so remains, while I'm left to ponder cultural preferences.

At the table, wherever I am, I speculate: What is this food saying? I wonder how it reveals place, time, people, dynamics. Looking back at the pomp and ceremony of our sumptuous family desserts, I glimpse my mother, Frankye, who loved grand gestures and *la bella figura,* slipping the cake server under a large piece and passing it to me, my father, my sisters, grandparents, and guests. In such a small town, in a time folded way back into memory, there I sit, already plotting a second piece later in the afternoon, not at all knowing that for my whole life, here's her gift: I always will be waiting for something spectacular.

. . .

Lemon Cheesecake

Preheat oven to 350 degrees.

> *½ pound butter, softened*
> *2 cups sugar*
> *2 eggs*
> *3 cups flour, sifted with the baking powder and salt*
> *2 teaspoons baking powder*
> *Pinch of salt*
> *1 cup buttermilk*
> *1 teaspoon vanilla*
> *4 egg whites, beaten*

- Beat together the butter and sugar, then beat in the eggs. Stir in the flour and milk alternately and beat for three to four minutes before folding in the vanilla and egg whites.
- Bake in two 9-inch pans, buttered and lined with parchment, for twenty-five minutes. Cool the cakes and unmold.

FILLING

> 2 cups sugar
> 4 tablespoons butter, softened
> 6 egg yolks, beaten
> 2 tablespoons flour
> 1 cup hot water
> Juice, about 9 tablespoons, and zest of three lemons

- Mix the sugar and butter well and beat in the yolks and flour. Add the liquids and cook in a double boiler until "it falls into flakes," stirring all the while. Cool. The filling should have the consistency of whipped cream.
- Spread the filling between the cake layers and on top, securing the layers with toothpicks if they start to slide.
- Frost the cake with a classic Seven-Minute White Icing.

. . .

Caramel Cake

Preheat oven to 350 degrees.

> 1½ cups sugar
> ¾ cup butter, softened
> 4 eggs
> 3 cups self-rising flour, sifted with the soda and salt
> ½ teaspoon baking soda

    ½ teaspoon salt
    1 cup buttermilk
    1 teaspoon vanilla
    1 teaspoon lemon juice

- Beat well the sugar and butter, then add the eggs one at a time. Fold in the flour mixture and the buttermilk alternately, lifting the batter to keep it light. Add the vanilla and lemon juice. Bake in buttered and lined 9-inch cake pans, for about twenty-five minutes, testing after twenty. Cool the cakes and remove from the pans.

RICH CARAMEL ICING

    1½ cups sugar
    1½ cups water
    4½ cups sugar
    2¼ sticks butter (18 tablespoons)
    1½ cups evaporated milk
    Pinch of salt
    1½ teaspoons vanilla

- On medium-low heat, add the cup of sugar and cup of water to a cast-iron skillet and cook them for twelve to fifteen minutes, stirring as the sugar dissolves, caramelizes, and turns light brown. Don't burn! Raise the heat to medium, and to the pan add the butter, evaporated milk, salt, and vanilla. Stir vigorously with a wooden spoon. After about five minutes, test the icing to see if it has reached the soft-boil stage; that is, drop a quarter teaspoon of the icing into a glass of tap water. If it forms a ball, it's ready. Continue to cook until this happens. Remove from the heat, beat another hundred strokes, then frost the first layer of the cake, top with the second, and frost all around.

FRANKYE'S
COOKBOOKS

SINCE I LEFT SAN FRANCISCO, WHERE I SPENT MY UNI-
versity teaching career, and relocated to the South, I am again
reveling in the food that my little silver spoon first dipped into
down in south Georgia, where everyone in my family knew,
and I soon would, too, that dinner, the midday meal, was the
event of the day, that Mr. Burnhart got melons in on Wednesday, corn every day of high summer, bushels of lady peas
infrequently—you had to reserve them—just-dug potatoes
from July on, and I came to know also that when Frankye, my
mother, pulled into the driveway with her boxes of fresh vegetables, Indian River grapefruits, and yellow plums, that
surely at the bottom I'd find several coconuts bought for her
triumphant three-layer coconut cake, partly to be achieved by
my contribution of hammering with an ice pick into the
"eyes" of the coconut, separating the "meat" from the cracked
shell, sections of which I formed into boats with sails made of
paper and toothpicks that would not stay glued but still served
as clumsy decorations around the cake as, borne aloft, it was
brought into the dining room after Sunday dinner, the ritual-
ized meal that only occasionally varied (perhaps a ham or
roast beef) from the fried chicken, rice and gravy, butter-

beans, biscuits, and depression-glass dishes of peach, watermelon rind, and bread-and-butter pickles, sharp hits of acidity to weigh in against crisp browned chicken, cream gravy, and the sugar bomb of dessert: pecan pie, lemon meringue, orange pound cake, lane cake, or the famous coconut with its soft, buttery layers, filling like whipped clouds and the crunch of fresh coconut reminding us, in scorching south Georgia, that somewhere dwelled the word *tropics*, some clime where the sun might be more demonic than here, where I often heard "dammit" from the kitchen as Mother endeavored to force egg whites to whip into meringue on a day when the humidity index tried to climb higher than 100 percent, causing the baked Alaska to fail, pie dough to clump, and cream to refuse to form peaks, and sending my mother to note in her Central Methodist Church cookbook: Do Not Attempt on a Humid Day, then to slam the book and shove it into the kitchen drawer that served as a library for her entire collection of cookbooks, an astonishingly meager array of two church missionary circle publications, "The Westinghouse Automatic Range Recipes," "The Knox Acidulated Gelatin Collection," a brochure from which nothing made it into her repertoire, "Meals Tested, Tasted, and Approved" from the Good Housekeeping Institute, and various refrigerator and baking powder brochures, all stuffed with yellowed and crumbling newspaper clippings, and the endpapers and blank spaces covered in Frankye's handwritten recipes, along with her other favorites written on the backs of checks, notepaper, stationery filched from the Sheraton Plaza Hotel in Daytona Beach, and hourly agenda pages torn from a life insurance daybook—that's it, the only records she kept, her magnificent talent for feeding us and friends and the sick and the dead's families recorded on paper scraps and interspersed with the books' absurd printed tips to wear long fur if you are tall and to carry a slender umbrella if you are stout, all of which I now keep (what would I grab if the house caught fire?) in my bookcase of four hundred cookbooks—how can it be: she remains the better cook—those totems of my thousands of dinner parties, holidays, celebrations, my great collection shelved with the basket holding her penciled, telegraphic words I always dive for when I long for her squash casserole (today), cane syrup pie, country captain chicken, or even better, classic chicken divan, wedding cookies dusted with powdered sugar, cheese biscuits, brown sugar muffins, corn pudding, or at Christmas when I recall most vividly her Martha Washington jetties, divinity, nutty fudge, bourbon balls, and peanut brittle, each recipe jotted down quickly, a minimalist document often omitting basic instructions, even ingredients, because she knew, and you should, too, you viewer of the long-ago activity in one seven-windowed, gaily café-curtained kitchen in the now-lost—good riddance—South, way back when I took for granted (and sat at the table with a hidden book open on my lap) as the door of the dining room swung open, as splendid platters appeared of smothered quail surrounded with fried potato croquettes, cornbread dressing stuffed inside the gleaming bronze turkey garlanded with cranberry swags, spoon bread, black bottom pie (recipe written in my older sister's aqua ink), brown sugar muffins—always the sweet contrast-to-salty offered at our table—oyster stew, spicy corn, marshmallow fudge cake, pressed chicken (I recognized this later in France as galantine), pork loin barbecued overnight on rusty mattress springs over a fiery pit and turned with a pitchfork, frozen fruit salad, chocolate icebox cake, Brunswick stew, tomato aspic, and always on my March birthdays, pink-frosted pound cake surrounded by white camellias—yes, all this, but no pasta, except sometimes spaghetti, no microgreens, bottarga, buratta, no sustainable New Zealand fish, few herbs, which I use copiously, no cheeses but cheddar and hoop cheese—my kitchen runs on Parmigiano—no artichokes, mangos, avocados, out-of-season grapes, no food processor, immersion blender, mandoline, parchment paper, nonstick pans, microplaner, ice maker, wire whisks, and no espresso maker, though Frankye did have an ice cream machine that I had to sit on to steady it when she cranked the handle, and she did have a meat grinder, a canning vat, and a Mixmaster so sturdy it probably would be running to this day if it had not been lost, as almost all else was lost, when my mother cooked no more, the yellow kitchen darkened and the house stood vacant, then suddenly sold so quickly that I salvaged only the cast-iron "spider" skillets and the recipes, not the rest, the small stash of tins where she stored paprika, Old Bay Seasoning, tarragon, mace, nutmeg, and red pepper flakes, gone, the pitcher for pineapple tea gone, the eggbeater, dented aluminum press for cheese straws gone, the timbale iron for savory fried rosettes to cover with chicken à la king gone, the angel food cake pan, the strawberry charlotte mold, all taken under the giant, oblivious blue wave that breaks hard when it breaks, then withdraws, pulling everything out far into the deceptive calm of memory, whose flood tides no moon can sway.

Summer Squash Casserole

A family favorite, squash casserole paired so well with the platter of fried chicken on the table at least once a week. Now I serve it with summer vegetable dinners— corn on the cob, tomato tarts, and big green salads. The original recipe used no olive oil, of course, and instead of the béchamel, my mother and aunts simply opened a can of cream of celery soup. I must say, it was delicious. In my zeal for nonprocessed food, I prefer to make the sauce. One of my favorite aspects of this dish is its sunny color.

Preheat oven to 350 degrees.

> *2 pounds yellow summer squash, thickly sliced*
> *3 tablespoons butter*
> *1 large onion, chopped*
> *2 tablespoons olive oil*
> *1 teaspoon salt*
> *½ teaspoon pepper*
> *2 tablespoons flour*
> *2 tablespoons butter*
> *1 cup whole milk*
> *3 eggs, beaten*
> *½ cup grated sharp cheddar*
> *¾ cup coarse bread crumbs, sautéed in 1 tablespoon*
> *   olive oil and seasoned to taste*
> *1 teaspoon of thyme, plus sprigs for the top*

- In a large pot, steam the squash until almost tender, about five minutes. Drain, mash with a fork, and dot with butter. Sauté the onion in olive oil until golden and translucent, about three minutes on medium-high heat. Stir the onion into the squash, and season with salt and pepper.
- In a small saucepan, prepare a béchamel sauce. Melt the remaining butter and stir in the flour, making a roux by gently cooking it on medium heat until well blended and just slightly beginning to brown. Remove from heat and whisk in the milk all at once. Return to low heat and stir until the sauce thickens nicely. Remove from the heat and whisk in the eggs, then stir the sauce into the squash. Add the cheese.
- Brown the bread crumbs in the same pan used for the onion and stir in the thyme. Mix most of the breadcrumbs into the squash and pour the mixture into a 9 x 12-inch buttered baking dish. Top with remaining crumbs and sprigs of thyme. Bake, uncovered, for twenty minutes and allow to cool slightly before serving.

Brown Sugar Muffins

Southern cuisine often features sweet breads at the dinner table, as well as the biscuits and rolls. My older sisters loved to whip up these delicate little muffins, especially when something salty such as ham was on the table. They're wonderful for breakfast.

Preheat oven to 350 degrees.

> *4 ounces butter*
> *1 cup light brown sugar*
> *1 egg, beaten*
> *2 cups all-purpose flour*
> *1 teaspoon baking powder*
> *1 teaspoon baking soda*
> *1 cup whole milk*
> *1 teaspoon vanilla*
> *½ cup chopped pecans*

- In a medium-size bowl, cream together the butter and sugar until light. Beat in the egg. Sift together the flour, baking soda, and baking powder, and add it alternately with the milk to the batter. Stir in vanilla and pecans. Pour the batter into a prepared pan for small muffins. Makes about eighteen. Test after ten minutes to see if tops are set.

Cheese Grits

We were always served grits for breakfast at my house, but I never appreciated them until I lived in Italy and learned all about polenta, the kissing cousin. Now I can't get enough of shrimp and grits, or of this Cheese Grits dish my mother used to make. Sometimes, when she served it with quail, she beat the egg whites separately, folded them in before turning the mixture into a baking dish, and called it Grits Soufflé.

Preheat oven to 350 degrees.

> *3½ cups water*
> *1 teaspoon salt*
> *½ teaspoon pepper*
> *1 cup stone-ground grits*
> *½ cup butter*
> *8 ounces sharp cheddar, grated*
> *1 cup whole milk*
> *4 eggs, beaten*

- In a large saucepan, boil the water with the salt and pepper, and add the grits gradually, stirring until they're blended. Cover the pot, turn the heat to low and simmer for twelve minutes, stirring now and then.
- Add the butter, cheese, and milk, and stir over low heat until the cheese and butter are melted. Beat in the eggs. Pour into a 2½-quart buttered dish and bake uncovered for thirty minutes. Serves ten.

Hot Corn

On the cob may be the preferred way, but I always have loved this spicy corn that you toss together in a black iron skillet, which, like the timbal iron, was called the "spider." The recipe calls for butter, of course, but I now use fresh, fruity olive oil. You can add yellow and green bell peppers and hot peppers if you want to up the heat. Sometimes I throw in baby okra or sliced zucchini or yellow squash. If you use a small jar of pimientos instead of a fresh one—they're not always easy to find—drain and add it at the end. If you're grilling chicken, this is a great summer side dish.

4 tablespoons butter
1 big onion, chopped
1 stalk of celery, diced
3 cups corn stripped from the cobs
1 pimiento or red bell pepper, diced
Grated peel of one lemon
¼ cup red wine vinegar
1 teaspoon Tabasco sauce
Dash of red pepper
2 cloves
1 tablespoon sugar
1 teaspoon salt
1 teaspoon pepper
½ cup heavy cream
Handful of parsley, chopped

- In a large skillet, melt the butter and sauté the onion and celery for about three minutes on medium heat. Add the corn and pimiento, stir, and keep cooking about five more minutes. Stir in the rest of the ingredients, except the parsley, turn heat to low, cover the skillet and simmer for another eight minutes. Remove the cloves and stir in the parsley. Serves six to eight.

Mary Davis's Cornmeal Dressing

At my aunt Mary's house, I learned that more is more. At the midday dinner, her round table off the kitchen was laden. Fried chicken and ham and a plethora of vegetables and mashed potatoes and my grandmother Big Mama Davis's biscuits, congealed salads, pitchers of tea, and pies. Not just one. Lemon and chocolate. Date roll and orange cake. Mary could flat-out cook. She was stuck with having blind and grouchy Big Mama live with her. (I never believed she couldn't see me sidling out of her reach.) The only thing on earth Big Mama didn't criticize was Mary's cooking, and Mary learned from her, so I guess she had some redeeming quality. When I started cooking in Italy, I appreciated Mary's stuffing for the Thanksgiving turkey more than ever. I had made it all my life without knowing of cornmeal's cousin, polenta. Forever after, I've added a cup or so of roasted chestnuts to Mary's dressing. Big Mama might or might not approve but who cares?

For a 12-pound turkey; halve this for a chicken:

1 cup cornmeal
2½ cups chicken stock
½ cup butter
1 cup chopped celery
½ cup chopped green bell pepper
1 chopped onion

Salt and pepper
1 teaspoon dried thyme
5 cups toasted bread cubes
2 eggs, beaten

- Combine cornmeal, stock, and butter in a large saucepan and cook on medium heat until it thickens, continuing to stir as it bubbles for about eight minutes. Add everything else. With a long spoon, stuff the bird as it's about to go in the oven. Or bake in a buttered 9 x 12 baking dish at 350 degrees for thirty minutes.

Country Captain Chicken

Suppers in the backyard often starred Country Captain, made with leftover fried chicken. This was transporting fare, since it included curry powder, a whiff of far-off and unimaginable India. The recipe yields lots of sauce for rice.

Makes 8 pieces of fried chicken.

Heat the oven to 350 degrees.

SAUCE

    2 tablespoons butter or bacon fat
    1 large onion, thinly sliced
    2 green bell peppers, chopped
    2 cloves garlic
    1 14-ounce can chopped tomatoes

Salt and pepper
2 teaspoons curry powder
1 tablespoon dried thyme
4 tablespoons currants
2 tablespoons sliced almonds
Handful of chopped parsley

- In a large skillet (one that can be covered and go in the oven), over medium-high heat, sauté the onion, peppers, and garlic until slightly browned, about three minutes. Add the tomatoes, seasonings, and currants. Blend and cook on medium heat for another five minutes. Mix in the chicken, cover, and bake for thirty minutes. Just before serving, stir in the almonds and parsley.

Tarragon Beans

My favorite of my mother's many green bean recipes. *Tarragon* seemed to me a beautiful word. Frankye got hers when we went to Atlanta, so unusual it was. The recipe specifies "salad oil." No thanks. Although I grew up with it, I wouldn't use it now, when healthy extra-virgin olive oil is available. (Then, olive oil came in a tiny bottle and seemed suspicious.) My mother crumbled bacon on top. If you want to, cook four or five strips of bacon in the microwave just before serving.

Serves 6–8.

1 ½ pounds of green beans, topped and tailed
2 tablespoons extra-virgin olive oil
1 large finely chopped onion

Steam the beans until just barely done. Meanwhile, in a medium skillet heat the olive oil and sauté the onion over medium-high heat until transparent, about three minutes. Stir in the beans and set aside.

DRESSING

¾ cup extra-virgin olive oil
½ teaspoon salt
1 teaspoon sugar
½ teaspoon paprika
2–3 shakes of red pepper
¼ teaspoon black pepper
¼ cup tarragon vinegar
juice and zest of 1 lemon
1 tablespoon fresh tarragon or ½ teaspoon dried
1 tablespoon fresh thyme or ½ teaspoon dried

• In a large bowl, whisk together all the dressing ingredients. Add the beans and onions to the bowl and toss well. Cover and let the beans marinate for three or four hours. Serve warmed or at room temperature. Crumble bacon on top if you choose.

AND AGAIN TO
THE GOLDEN ISLES

✦

I AM GOING TO A SMALL HAWAIIAN ISLAND FOR FIVE DAYS.
Walk, swim, read, eat pineapple and grilled fish—a simple
break. I will hear lulling waves in my sleep, feel the balm of
wind that has crossed over water, see the whole ball of the sun
drop behind the blue-penciled horizon every day. These expectations dip under tectonic plates of my oldest memories,
touching the early experience of living on the Georgia Sea
Islands in summer.

Last spring, I took one of the little boats that ply the waters of the Venetian lagoon. With Venice shimmering across
milky green water, I kept my face in the wind for the salty,
iodine smell of marshes, and the bare emergence from the
water of the scattered reedy islands, which seem to have no
time scale, a serious warping of perspective. Landing on Tor-
cello, Erasmo, then others, I had the feeling that all inhabitants had fled hundreds of years ago. Still, the islands remained
themselves. This experience, too, made that plumb line dip
into deep-heart memory.

Hawaii and the Venetian islands thrill me but the real islands, the prototypical, archetypal, metabolic, medulla-lodged
islands are those off the coast of Georgia.

"They're at the island," I still can hear my mother saying into the telephone, or "We won't be back from the island until August." Packed into the Oldsmobile with my two sisters, our cook, Willie Bell, record players and hairdryers in their zip cases, toys, clothes, and my mother (my father was driven separately to avoid our chaos), I leaned out the window like a dog, my hair springing into curls, waiting for the first scent. Even the word *island* symbolized summer and freedom. Every morning I was out on the beach alone when the sun came wobbling out of the water. I took a forbidden swim alone. The beach was perfect for cartwheeling until I was dizzy.

Every few years, I'm pulled back to those Georgia islands my mother's voice evokes. I need to see the marshes, which imprinted on me. The beach at Sea Island was the first landscape I knew I loved. When we left, I wouldn't speak all the way back to Fitzgerald. The marshes, not land, not sea. This was where I knew I always would belong.

Little St. Simons: The seven-mile beach looks as empty as it did on the day of creation. A knot unties as I walk as far as I can see along the edge of the Atlantic. Green water on my left, beach and dunes on my right. Unparalleled Robinson Crusoe beach. Where's Friday? No buildings in sight—no houses, condo complexes, no mini-marts or golf carts, no high-rise, highway, not even another lone walker. Only three pelicans for companionship. The beach is strewn with shells— angel wings, scallops, sand dollars, and thousands of conchs, both white and the bluish pink swirled ones with all the colors of sunset inside. I pick up dozens, discarding them as I find perfect specimens, then give up and leave them all in the sand.

Sky: enormous. Ocean: endless. Beach: feet were formed to walk on this sand.

I wander back to the hotel on a one-and-a-half-mile trail through the marshes, spotting an alligator with a baby one on her back lolling in the brackish water just off the raised path, and an armadillo in full knight's armor scurrying into the sea myrtle. Vines and moss drape the live oaks. Except for the breeze rattling the palmettos and the squawk of a seabird or two, silence.

This is one of Georgia's Golden Isles, a necklace of islands strung all along the coast. Although my family rented houses on Sea Island and St. Simons, I now adore the idyllic isolation of Little St. Simons, inaccessible to cars.

When I was a child, nearby Jekyll Island was abandoned. Because *The Swiss Family Robinson* was a favorite book, I was riveted by the idea of a deserted island of twisted oaks hung with moss. Finally, my sister and her boyfriend agreed to go, and we rowed over from St. Simons. They are off on their own and I explore the empty mansions of "fool Yankee robber barons," as Daddy called them, which had been left with swimming pools full of algae and French doors to terraces open and swaying in the breeze. I find letters on closet shelves in empty rooms and flowered pieces of broken china on the kitchen floors. Jekyll today is transformed into a state park, teeming, at times, with tourists. The small brick ranch houses of the 1960s begin to take on a historic air. The mansions are renovated, repurposed. I must lift off this present overlay to recover the wild island I knew, and the complex past I did not know then. One of the last American boats bringing captured Africans to a future of enslavement landed on the south shore of Jekyll in 1858. A museum on the island is dedicated to the history of the *Wanderer*, a pleasure boat turned slave ship, and to the captured Africans who landed here. Long after, northern mega-rich built their enormous "cottages" and came to escape brutal winters. By the 1970s, small ranch houses dotted the quiet island. The loudest sound was mosquitoes. My first memory: a listing dock, where our red boat tied up. Long after the agony and frivolity, I leapt out, exited to roam alone.

Some of the Georgia barrier islands are nature preserves or, like Cumberland, partly private. For decades, the same family of pencil manufacturers owned Little St. Simons. They bought it for the cedar but found the island trees too twisted for pencil making. By then they'd fallen in love with the island. Their home later became an intimate inn. Fortunately, you can imagine that it's yours.

The few guests seem to be bird-watchers. At the family-style meals, much talk is of the green herons spotted that afternoon, newly hatched egrets, or osprey nests. The last thing I want to do is spy on birds, but I'm grateful that this is one of the top sanctuaries for the winged on the east coast. With most of the guests glued to their field glasses, I have to myself the perfect beach, the big turquoise swimming pool, and even the horse trails. Sitting on the porch, I am visited by an albino deer who folds herself up at my feet and goes to sleep. I freeze: In this moment I am the heroine in a fairy tale.

Late, when the sun angles across the marsh, my daughter and I take a canoe and paddle slowly among the reeds, half enchanted by the reflected sky on the water and half terrified that a gator will rise from the depths and tip us into its jaws. Nights are for the stars. Living in a city, it's easy to forget the heavens. In this complete dark, there they are blazing away. The constellations hum like electrical pylons in a field. No, those are mosquitoes. Could they lift me and carry me to bed?

DO ISLANDS EXIST IN the landscape the same way memories exist in the mind—is that the source of their lure? Solid hunks of reality surrounded by seas. What's forgotten, lost, irretrievable? Are there land- and seascapes you have no choice but to call home, even if you are only visiting for three days?

I found one shell in my pocket when I came home from Little St. Simons, a small conch, dawn-colored. It's in my desk drawer, and when I take out a pen, I sometimes rub inside the gleaming nacreous curve. Just a touch pulls me under. Marshes, islands, lagoons—the ancient places where water will have its way.

IV

MOMENTARY
HOMES

THE CURIOUS ARE ALWAYS IN SOME DANGER.
IF YOU ARE CURIOUS,
YOU MIGHT NEVER COME HOME . . .

—*Jeanette Winterson,*
Oranges Are Not the Only Fruit

Why Not Stay

❧

IN *GIRO*, ITALIAN WORDS I LIKE. ALSO *GITA*, A LITTLE TRIP. *In giro* amounts to a philosophy for me—traveling. In my jewelry drawer, I have a brooch from the 1930s that says, in swirly script, *Va e Torna*, go and return. Often, I pick it up and contemplate: *Where next?*

Some reasonable and sensitive people don't have the gene for travel. A college friend traveled to Europe our sophomore year. I couldn't wait to hear of her adventures, but when she returned she said, "I'm so glad I went. Now I don't ever have to go again."

Between the manic traveler and the homebody, others feel the frequent urge to strike out for foreign climes. In 1386, Geoffrey Chaucer introduced *The Canterbury Tales* with the conviction that when winter ends "thane longen folk to goon on pilgrimages." Yes, we still so long to go. Surely travel was rougher back then (brigands, fleas, carriages stuck in mud), though we feel incensed over crowds, airports, and delays, as though travel should be smooth and easy. In this current period of unrest for travelers, even we manic travelers must stop and consider.

I left North Carolina as my lemonade-colored hyacinths

bloomed. The rare yellow magnolia had just burst forth with its hand-width flowers. The basil and zinnia seeds broke through the soil with determination. My new computer seemed to make writing a breeze. With fresh blue-and-white comfortable chairs and a stack of good books in my study, I hated to depart. Though I'm torn, on balance I tip just slightly toward the airport. Always, I have the fierce urge to *go,* just go.

In late March sunshine, we landed in Rome, proceeded through customs and out into the usual swarm at Fiumicino Airport. Immediately, Ed headed to the bar for a deep hit of espresso before we started the two-hour journey to our house in Cortona. Once in the rented car, I snapped my Italian chip into my phone and the news of bombs—where? Brussels?— began to pour across the screen. Just as we had touched down, the explosions had happened. We navigated mad traffic; it's so easy to miss that right turn to the north and get lost in some hinterland of Rome. After a seventeen-hour sleepless, turbulent trip, we were intent on finding our way home. The news seemed unreal; how is this happening again?

We arrived in a heap, exhausted, but thrilled to see the wild double daffodils on our hillside, the hawthorn bushes a haze of white, and that sweet view of the greening valley below our house. What a boon—our fine friend Gilda left some roasted artichokes, and her silky *panna cotta.* After a long, jet-lagged nap, we unpacked quickly, popped open a bottle of wine, and threw together a pasta with tomato sauce and lots of herbs.

A guttering candle, a full moon out the window, good Italian music playing—the peace of home. "Why," I asked Ed, "do we keep traveling? All this hassle . . . someone frisking you at security."

"Do you want to stay at home—read, cook, garden, see friends, take walks, write?"

"Yes. No, but I'm tired of travelers' yellow alerts, drug-sniffing dogs all over airports. And there's random danger. Remember Karie looked the wrong way in London and got hit by a potato chip truck. We could just vacation two hours away at the beach."

"You were restless after three days when we rented that lake house. That stuff could happen anywhere. You could fall off a ladder at home. You love Turkey and Greece and Mexico. There are always waves of trouble. This will pass."

I get the last word. "I'm not often on a ladder." He's right. I'm temporarily thrown. The world does not cradle us, does not spread beautifully at the feet of those of us who thrive on travel. But hell, has it ever?

The great writer Freya Stark said: "To awaken quite alone in a strange town is one of the pleasantest sensations in the world." Thinking of this brave pilgrim, who was the first foreign woman to venture into Syria, Arabia, and other far-flung places in the 1920s, revives my own passion. What spurred her toward the ancient incense roads and the camel caravan tracks across remote deserts? These are questions I puzzle over while reading her magnificent books. One small kernel: ". . . a passion for mystery chiefly which explains the optimism of human beings towards . . . travel." Yes, who are those unknown others out there, and how do they live? Always the question: Could I live here? What's home like here?

How many times I've relished the private thrill of a foreign place where you know no one, speak a handful of words, where even the street signs throw you off balance. How you feel your mind open to the new. How you set forth, all synapses crackling with curiosity.

The sensation of being in the Alhambra in Granada comes back often. I expected to be interested, but I did not expect to be moved by the place. (Memory, let me walk there again.) I love the colored tiles, stonework carved as finely as lace, splashing fountains and serene pools with the illusion of coolness that the Moors loved. Love the perspectives through arches, and the twelve marble lions, each of which spouts water on its hour of the day. Memory lets me sit in the garden listening to Manuel de Falla's *Nights in the Gardens of Spain,* one of those moments in travel when the complex layers of history, beauty of place, and the sense of yourself as *there* coalesce. Traveler, you feel the place as an electric current running down your spine.

By dessert, we're already discussing summer travel plans with our family. Circles on the map: Napoli, Torino, Genova, Firenze. My next project will be a book about hidden Italian small towns, so my travel will expand exponentially. Already I have folders and notebooks and files on places I want to see.

Still, there's caution on the wind. Uncertainty remains certain. But we can't be in thrall to the unknown. My family is excited by the plan for a few days in Napoli in hot July. Napoli, a warned-against city, is one of my favorite places. What will befall us? I expect sublime sea views and pizza, vibrant street food and fish markets, stunning artifacts from Pompeii in the museum, seeing a family of four on a single Vespa careening through the streets. I expect to be awed. And I anticipate that rush of excitement when I take my laptop to a park bench and try to find words adequate to the experience of being there.

The road less traveled; the journey, not the arrival matters; go west—all the old saws are true but perhaps the essayist and memoirist Anaïs Nin says it most viscerally: "I'm restless. Things are calling me away. My hair is being pulled by the stars again." Travel is like that, the magnetic pull toward a moment, somewhere in Peru or Morocco or Slovenia where you collide with an essence of the place. Travel is a privilege because it gives you the world you were not given. It allows you to be extant in other versions.

I sat on a rocky beach on a Turkish island. Five little girls selling scarves came over to show their mothers' work, cotton wisps edged with pearls, in all the soft colors. Their pet goat tried to nibble my toes. The girls wound the scarves around me, played with my hair, leaned against me, laughed, and brought me pretty stones. They are with me still. Should I have stayed at home?

BLUE APRON

A LONG, LONG TIME AGO, BEFORE GLORIOUS FARMERS'
markets bloomed, before the nonstop master chefs, recipe
blogs, and home cake makers trying not to look foolish
on bake-offs, before the proliferation of excellent food websites, before foams that can look like spit, gluten crazes, sous
vide, before food became cult, and way before every third
mas, villa, and farm kitchen in France and Italy became a
cooking school, I journeyed far to study with Simone Beck in
sun-soaked Provence.

What propelled me across the Atlantic in those dim years?
My (former) husband was sailing all the time he was not
working. I was manning the jib and raising the spinnaker and
cooking in the gimbaled kitchen, not with much pleasure except when we anchored off Angel Island for the night and saw
the deer come down to drink from the caretaker's sprinklers
and we lit candles along the bow and sat under the stars
drinking wine. Otherwise, the wind was capricious and often
vicious, San Francisco Bay surprisingly shallow in spots,
causing us to run aground when the sonar wasn't working,
which it often wasn't. Then we waited for the tide to change.
Sharks raised their mugs along the boat's edge. If I fell asleep,

the dreams were of a whale lifting us into the air and plunging us into the frigid waters.

Often, I felt that I was flying around my room, a bird come down through the chimney. My daughter was entranced with her horse. We constantly prepared grainy meals for Chelsea, bought off the racetrack and incorrigible. I wanted to be a writer but kept cooking instead. Go somewhere new, I thought. My friend Jeannette called to tell me about the cooking classes in sun-drenched Provence, and before she finished the sentence, I said, "Let's go."

We were five at Simone "Simca" Beck's honey-colored house, La Campanette, in the hills above Grasse: Jeannette, also from the Bay Area, two pretty and accomplished young women from Atlanta, and a mysterious woman from South Africa who was sent there while her boyfriend went on vacation with his wife. Jeannette and I had devoured *Mastering the Art of French Cooking*, which Simca co-authored with Julia Child. We were adept at dinner parties featuring cream soups, Veal Prince Orloff, Grand Marnier Soufflé, and other time-consuming, flamboyant recipes. We loved *Simca's Cuisine*, her straightforward approach, and immediately liked her no-nonsense rigor in the kitchen. On the first day, she gave each of us an apron that matched her impression of us. Mine was plain blue, while the others got charming flowers and stripes. Simca was cordial to us, but not friendly. When Cathy from Atlanta asked one question too many, Simca cut her off with "Are we going to measure, or are we going to cook?" That terse reply became a mantra for me. We worked in the morning, and then enjoyed a sumptuous lunch on the terrace. Fish mousseline with hollandaise, pizza with pastry crust, poached sole in a ring mold with velouté, and various sausages in brioche—not exactly Sunday night suppers but still easy and fun. Simca demonstrated. We were assigned small tasks. We took notes. We did not clean up.

If one of us asked a question she usually looked incredulous through her tinted glasses and curtly said, "But you have it in de *Mastering*," as if we should have memorized the whole tome. But I was learning how to beat egg whites in a copper bowl until I could hold the bowl upside down over my head— that's how you know they're stiff enough. I learned to cook chicken stock uncovered so that it reduces and concentrates. We made an airy rolled soufflé filled with crab. Never brown shallots, just melt them. She preferred metal spoons because wooden ones "always have some fat on them." I learned to keep my knives sharp and dry. Never waste anything. I saw her save the whites when only yolks were needed. Leftover bread became crumbs. Shells of shrimp went into the broth. From that plain kitchen, I brought home life-changing habits. Many small changes add up to revolutionary change. She respected ingredients as a writer respects words. Frugal as she was, the table was set with largesse. Her trucs and scoldings and care gently seeped into my hands and made me more aware as I stood at the stove. I began to see the process of cooking as an art and a practice, not a means to an end. I began to love the battered pans, wooden bowls, a particular slotted spoon, colanders, and baskets. My tools.

French desserts descended to earth from a certain corner of heaven. We constructed then devoured Simca's toffee-based tart of packed-down apples *(tartin des pommes)*, chocolate gateau garnished with cherries in kirsch, and a dense chocolaty-chocolate mousse without cream. She taught the French way with meringue—cook it over hot water then, through a pastry tube, pipe decorative rings around fruit or lemon tarts. (Way too much trouble.)

I could not know that, from Simca's dessert repertoire, one recipe would come to stand for all the tastes, aromas, and bliss of my time at La Campanette—Le Diabolo, a flat, dense, unassuming chocolate cake. Simca took the recipe from her mother's little black notebook. I recall vividly the first taste: the inner essence of chocolate, sweet and bitter, a touch of almond, and buttery with a slight hit of darkness from the coffee in the chocolate spread on top. A complex cake, I thought. I don't know if I'd ever made a complex cake before. The ones I knew were straightforward, except for my mother's formidable lane cake, which I'd attempted once with no success.

The name, too, is complex. I assumed *diabolo* meant "devil." But a French devil is *diable*. Italian and Spanish devils are *diavolo* and *diablo*. Going way back to the Greek, a *diabolos* was a liar. For later Christian writers, the word meant "the liar who speaks against God," therefore, a devil. I can see why one might think of that deep chocolate as diabolical, as in *the devil made me do it*. But why Simca's mother spelled her cake *diabolo* remains a mystery, and we can't ask now. Perhaps it's dialect or an obsolete spelling. Maybe she liked juggling, because now the word *diabolo* refers to a nifty device for a juggler's tricks, a sort of double cup joined at the bottom and strung between two sticks. When we separated eggs, Simca taught us to break the shell, turn the egg into our hands, letting the whites slip through our fingers while the yolks remained whole in our palms. "You must be very sure of your eggs," she cautioned. Cooking can be a bit like juggling.

Made in a round baking pan, the ancient devil stands two inches high, at most. Although in her cookbook Simca lists an American chocolate, you can be sure that in her French kitchen she used chocolate from a special shop in Paris. Little flour is called for, and ground almonds keep the batter from ambitious rising. The top becomes slightly crusty and the middle stays moist—more than moist, but not quite creamy. "You must not overbake," she warned. One minute past noon is midnight, some writer said, and that's true here. The soft and delectable texture can turn dry and brittle in a flash.

As soon as it cools, you pour over it a simple coffee-based chocolate butter cream, thin but intense. Guests put down their forks and look at you as though you've unveiled *The Winged Victory*. A sliver will do—this is not the same thing at all as the much-loved towering layer 1-2-3-4 cakes of my youth. They were slathered in luscious thick icing. Discovering Le Diabolo was sort of like the moment of recognition when you're dressed in blue flounces and someone wearing black Prada walks in. You get it.

When something is this good, you don't need much. Sometimes I ring the cake with raspberries, but, really, what's the point? Le Diabolo needs no embellishment. In my kitchens, I have turned out Le Diabolo onto the same white Wedgwood plate for my daughter's birthdays, endless dinner parties, potlucks, even funerals. Now my daughter bakes it for her family, and I've passed on the recipe to many friends, who, in turn, have handed it to others. I could write the recipe on my kitchen walls. On that first day, however, my history with Le Diabolo was unwritten. I ate each bite slowly, slowly, savoring every rich morsel.

In the afternoons, we meandered to Biot, Fayence, Vence. We were allowed in the kitchens of the Michelin-starred chefs in the area. We flirted with Paul Bocuse. Sharp-eyed Simca took us to markets and taught us to buy the right fish—look at its eyes and the shimmer of the scales—and cunning little cheeses wrapped in grape leaves, and olives, and small purple artichokes. We learned to drink kir royale (and I'd thought Champagne was glamorous) on the terrace at evening, where, with Simca and her husband, Jean, we were sometimes joined by Julia herself and her courtly husband, Paul. The effervescent sunset light in the kir seemed to have absorbed the color of the rays raking across the distant hills. Julia was interested in how we "girls" were getting on. Her high voice thrilled us, and although we were shy around her, we had fun trying to imitate her when we were back in our quarters.

PARALLEL TO THE EXCITEMENT in the kitchen, I was seduced by the gentle landscape. Blowing across the flowering fields was the bright new idea of a life in the countryside. The air was balm. The mornings, when I took early walks, stunned me with their sweetness. As we drove, I was dazzled by golden, perched villages, the Matisse chapel, and the acres of roses cultivated by perfume makers. We sometimes stopped, as evening fell, at a small square and dined outdoors under plane trees. Biting into *poulet à l'estragon*, it was easy to savor the way of life behind the genuine food. *I'd like to live this way.*

The trip was brief. Poppies spread like brushfire all over

the fields. Never had I seen such a marvel. How is it that some people get to live their everyday lives here? I fancied as I packed my bag that I could fold into my clothes the scent of the nearby roses. Simca's book was dog-eared and spattered. Provençal fabric sacks of pungent herbs penetrated all my summery dresses. En route back to the States, on a stop in Paris, I madly purchased a copper bowl for whipping egg whites, chocolate (grocery store chocolate was over), individual cylindrical molds for soufflés d'Alençon, vanilla powder, various extracts, a nutmeg grinder, and all sizes of tart pans, some of which, eons later, still have the stickers on them. Who knew when I'd ever pass that way again?

I went home. Even a short trip can shift your perspective. My family had come first, first, and first. Simca summed up a feeling I was inching toward when she asked, "Are we going to measure or are we going to cook?" I enrolled in graduate school. The faculty asked me to stay on and teach. I became a writer. Then, imagine, chair of the department. Years after, I bought a honey- and rose-colored house on a hillside in Tuscany, where I love to cook and entertain my friends. I grow roses. The view to the south falls away into olive and grape terraces, and a small tower anchors the distant hills. I must have baked Simca's chocolate cake five hundred times.

FRAGMENTS

I was not searching for anything or anyone,
I was searching for everything, searching for everyone.

—OCTAVIO PAZ

⚷

WHEN I LOOKED OUT THE WINDOW AND SAW A PILGRIMAGE line of bare-chested men flagellating themselves with rope whips, I knew I was in surreal territory. Fine with me. Octavio Paz, the Mexican writer, said that here surrealism runs in the streets. My marriage was in shreds, and our Palo Alto home about to be sold. What better solution than to rent a poet friend's house in San Miguel de Allende for the summer and see if any clarity emerged. The two-story white stucco house, square on a corner of Recreo and a narrow lane, was filled with books, handwoven textiles, pre-Columbian pottery, and mice.

Across the lane, flocks of snowy egrets nested in the swaying tops of trees, and catty-cornered below was the dusty Benito Juarez Park, where women still washed their clothes in a stone trough. Let the marriage burn off me, I thought. I will translate myself into a new language.

I made friends with a woman who had a child by a matador, but she did not tell the father. My daughter and niece took classes and flirted with Mexican boys who sometimes gathered under the windows imploring the "blondies" to come out. A stream of friends from home visited and left. I didn't say I'd seen a mouse run under the guest bed at night. I bought armfuls of tuberoses that scented the hot rooms. A man on a donkey delivered milk from a tin jug. A strand of brown straw floated on top. I bought a pail then poured it out. All of us loved the thermal springs, the dressed-up mummies in Guanajuato, the promenade in *el jardín* at evening, the spare beauty of Querétaro. I liked riding rickety yellow buses with tin crosses and bleeding hearts and Madonnas dangling from the rearview mirror, torch music blaring.

Every day for five hours I went to Spanish class. My teacher, Raoul, was a small man in cowboy boots with kitten heels. Soon we became friends and started taking field trips to practice Spanish in larger settings. He had a friend with a low-down taxi who drove us to old churches with elaborately painted walls—and more pilgrims whipping themselves. I bought one of the knotted ropes in case I had the urge. We stopped at stands selling roasted corn with lime. We drove off-road, through hard fields, and searched for Chichimeca fragments. I found a terra-cotta plate with only a pie-slice piece missing. My Spanish, I thought, was becoming fluent.

One day, crossing an abandoned cemetery, I saw four boys playing. Their ball was a human skull. Other smashed skulls and bones lay scattered about and a stray dog crunched on, what, a tibia? As the skull punted past me, I grabbed it and ran. One minute later, it would have been smithereens. When I got home, I saw permanent teeth embedded above the baby teeth. The baby's fontanel was not yet closed, the black lines like jagged stitching on a shroud, like the EKG of a suspicious heart, or the tracing of an uncertain economy. I placed it in the bookshelf, on top of its countrymen Octavio Paz's and Jaime Sabines's books of poems.

Raoul began to confess that he was trapped, would never get out of teaching Spanish to people like me who only visited like locusts in season. He cried over the fate of the Chichimeca people and took me to more stubbled corn fields to look for pottery. The trunk of his car rattled with the fragments. The house behind mine was torn down and droves of mice exited the foundations. When I came downstairs one morning, the kitchen counters were covered in hundreds of mice. I ran upstairs, screaming. Then Maria, the housecleaner, came in clapping her hands and shouting for poison. At the market we bought a brown bottle marked with skull and crossbones. We cleaned the house until the tiles gleamed and the wood shone. We stuffed steel wool in every crevice.

I was in love with Mexico, the zigzag gaiety and sudden parades and the scents and thumps of tortilla making, the powerful indigenous art, the sensibility that formed candies into skeleton shapes, the outrageous fuchsia bougainvillea, the plaintive guitars. I was dazzled by the colors and music and beneath those I felt a current of stoicism and melancholy. With my own life in shards, the pottery hunts felt like huge metaphors. I would not find the piece that completed the Chichimeca plate. This would not become my home but a place to return to in imagination all my life. Then, I needed to go back to California and take on my new reality. My Spanish wasn't so good. After the lists of verb conjugations and vocabulary words, I wrote a line from Sabines in my notebook: *Let's see what sort of image of yourself you make out of the pieces of your shadow you pick up.* I still wonder about Raoul, poking through the weeds among startled goats. What has he found?

A Place to Hide

FOR WORKING ON A CREATIVE PROJECT, THE BLISSFUL island climate imparts a godlike joy. Waking to the scent of orange blossoms and temperature that says, *You're mine, don't worry, I always will caress you like this*—the book I am writing seems natural. The fragrant air makes me feel rocked in the cradle.

It's seventy-five degrees and cloudless. The blue dome of sky resembles an inverted glazed, cobalt, china teacup. The island is a maze of cunning paths. Soon I am on not a walk but a hike, down, down, down. The mind goes plunging, happily, scarily, vertiginously. The colors of the water remind me of some of my favorite flowers—lobelia, delphinium, and a particular pansy the color of the sky on a starry night.

The houses offer views of the ideal life—long walks with silence, with mesmerizing scents of flowers, swims in a transparent sea layered with emerald, lapis, turquoise water. Move into one of the domed houses and soon you would be painting the walls blue, setting a pot of basil by the door to keep out the bugs, and napping away the hot hours under an arbor. Or writing a novel.

Lentisk, prickly pear, pine, asphodel, myrtle. Perhaps they

were planted by the gods. I think after six months here I might emerge, finally, as a disciplined writer. I would certainly emerge with iron calf muscles. The outsider's solitude and loneliness breed fantasy. Could not a sea monster arise from the waves, the ghosts of all those women abducted by pirates not cry out from the rocks? Maybe I would finish my abandoned long poem.

One of Capri's primordial appeals must be the scale. In a lifetime at home here, you could know the island as well as you know the loved one's body. Know each carob, every stone wall with dangling capers, all the outbreaks of yellow broom, all caves and coves.

The surprise: The touristy island offers a large solitude. What comprises the essence of this place? The guides don't tell me. But the waves on the rocks tell me, the fisherman's blue shirt shouts it out, the delicate shadow of an almond tree on a white wall scrawls three reasons in black. Capri— combing the island, inhaling sun-baked scents of wild mint, lemon, and the sea, making love in a mother-of-pearl light, joking with the woman chopping weeds along her fence, memorizing a tumble of pink and apricot passion vine intertwining on a white wall, picnicking on a pebble beach, leaning to catch a hot grape I toss toward my open mouth.

Who could resist a chance to live here, to be that topless girl reading Derrida on the beach, the young boy diving off the rocks, the ageless woman hanging an octopus on the clothesline. You could live here, you could.

Water Maze

Venice, a state of mind. The scintillating, kaleidoscopic, shifting colors of that aqueous realm remain alive inside me long after I depart the city. While there, the sensory overload leaves me happily exhausted at the end of day, reeling with images of the man peeling artichokes at fifty miles an hour in the Rialto market, stalls mounded with lurid fish, clothes waving on lines strung across canals, squadrons of pigeons, the flashing oars of the gondoliers, the lure of luxury shops, the shadowy windows of the *ombra* (shadow) bars, tourists gorging into San Marco, narrow streets leading me farther into a labyrinth, even the sparrows pecking at my bread basket at a waterside restaurant. I let myself wander all day, following a glimpse of a facade, a snatch of violin music, a child kicking a ball, and a cascade of blue plumbago hanging over a distant garden wall. I'm almost thoughtless in Venezia (after you're there, it's Venice no longer), reverting to a primitive creature who takes on the color and temperature of where I sit, sipping a spritzer in an ocher, apricot, and stone piazza.

Mysterious. Venezia feels like the maze of my psyche. I follow the squares, turns, bridges, canals, looking for signs,

omens. Eventually the city, I'm certain, will lead to some secret X I've sought all my life.

Later and far away from Venezia, the city floating through
memory is silent. It belongs only to me, the traveler. I stand
again in Palladio's Il Redentore, watching that white-as-
icicles light fall through the lofty coved windows. Was the
cold light a part of his architectural plan? In a city patched
from an *abbondanza* of tints and hues, did he think: *You shall
be immersed in white air?* I step outside and the Grand Canal—
suddenly still—has darkened under a cloud to shimmering
blue, like the supple Venetian velvet cape I once glimpsed on
a woman stepping off a yacht in the rain. (If I ever saw another, I'd mortgage my house to buy it.) But maybe it's
enough, just to remember an expanse of water faceted with
light. Venezia, the literal gate to the earliest home, the watery
subconscious. Under an arched bridge, the narrow canal—
what is that green? Liquid malachite? The eyes of the first
boy I loved . . . Yes, and when the sun hits, the color shifts to
the green of a parrot's wing. At lunch, nearby motor launches
break up the surface, cutting the reflections into cubist angles
of blue, yellow, red, and white, churning and reforming.

At night, the reflections turn silver and gold; long wands
of starry shapes easily mesmerize me. Always in memory, the
moon is full. Nowhere is the moon as powerful, enormous,
so . . . well, heavenly. Because it floats, the city floats, too, becomes a mirage of a mirage. The moon could be chipped from
travertine by an artist. Why not? Haven't humans created this
unlikely phantasm of a city? Couldn't they just as easily hang
a moon over it?

On the brink of sleep, I sense the light in the Carpaccio

painting at the Gallerie dell'Accademia, *The Dream of Saint Ursula*. She is sleeping with her little dog at her bedside. At the door, the angel has just arrived, holding the palm of her martyrdom. He steps into the room in a triangle of sunlight. All these years, that golden light has fallen into the calm bedroom where she is dreaming. The memory of a place is like that. You are the dreamer. You are the room. You open the door over and over.

V

FRIENDS
AT HOME

HOME-MADE, HOME-MADE! BUT AREN'T WE ALL?

—Elizabeth Bishop

FRIENDSHIP IS ALL THE HOUSE I HAVE.

—William Butler Yeats

HOME THOUGHTS:
A LITANY

*Having a Coke with You is even more fun than going
to San Sebastian, Irún, Hendaye, Biarritz . . .*

—FRANK O'HARA

WHEN I MISS MY FRIENDS, I MISS THEIR HOMES, TOO.
And their porch fans, garden gates, pergolas, fern-filled
sunrooms—where they live their lives. I often walk through
their houses, especially when I'm thousands of miles away.
Every room resonates with my friends' presence, as though
I've made a memory palace of their homes. Foyer with thirty
mirrors, fireplace constantly blazing, creaky stair landing,
back hall full of boots, but above all the dining room, where
we've gathered for quick lunches, feasts, holidays. I can see
my friend enter, smiling, the coq au vin or the soup tureen
held aloft. Studies and living rooms—all the book launches,
wedding (even divorce) celebrations, and birthdays. Political
fundraisers and book groups and writing groups or just an
evening of movies. Their rooms reveal: a sense of humor or
gloom, pretentions, solitude, exuberance, introversion, or
longing for light.

What an intimate act, to invite someone into your home.

There's Steven, in situ. Three Stevens! Judy, Jackie, Debbie, Ondine, Coco, Silvia. They flash in memory framed by where they live, never more vivid than in their rooms. I'm touching their things chosen from travels, the collections (glass sea buoys, julep cups, vintage matchbooks from Paris, aluminum colanders—weird stuff!), fabrics, kitchen knobs, desks cluttered or precise. Even their closets. Are Aziz's socks ironed? Although some of the friends I conjure in memory no longer exist, the green glass lamp still shines on Bill's desk where he wrote poems. From under the bed, a glimpse of his blond wig. Don't ask. I can see the view of three bridges from Jackie's top floor and push aside Judy's student papers from her kitchen table so we can sip her bergamot tea. My lost friends' rooms return them to me briefly and also bounce back my own sense of home. I walk the rooms of houses I've lived in. What became of the coral sofa, the rolltop desk, the blue-and-white plates?

Objects become illuminated. They speak Robin, they speak Toni and Shotsy, they speak Michele. Like saints' palm fronds, dogs, keys, scallop shell, lion, book, my friends in their private havens have their attributes. Make a home and it will say who you are and maybe why. Objects chosen, displayed, cared for, they're like the salt, milk, wine, dishes, and lamps that Romans offered to the lares, household gods.

On an insomniac night, I see Ippy stepping out onto her back porch for a moment of overlooking the pond. When she and Neil had a book party for me, a neighbor boy rowed a young flautist in a yellow canoe across the pond and the silvery music and the apparition of the girl in white standing in the canoe reached everyone sipping wine in the yard. We hushed. From the front, the dark wooden house lies low, as serene and austere as a Japanese *ryokan*. The facade looks closed and gives nothing away. You announce your arrival with a thump to a gong, which still reverberates when the door flings open. The back, all windows, faces Frog Level Pond. Ippy, on her porch, may now be seeing that drifting canoe scene. She slides the door and goes into the house. Clean lines, watery light, gray cat, bold art on every wall, some of the paintings hung way lower than eye level just to make you see. She's headed for her studio, intent, but I stop her in the living room. This audacious choice. Against a wall of windows filled with blond light, a long, curvy, sexy velvet sofa. Pink. Pale pink. Surely she was told it is *too much,* she'll tire of the color, powder-puff pink, pink as a mimosa blossom, pink as the nacreous inside of a shell. She won't. She lives with certainty and originality. When I go to Ippy's house, I feel lifted as soon as she opens the door. The house is all her and the welcome is palpable.

To get to Jane's, I turn off and bump and jounce until I come to a yard full of odd bits that may be placed or maybe have been dropped. Carts, statues, twisted iron sculptures (or just twisted cast-off iron), pots with long-dead agave and aloe plants. And there's Jane in the kitchen. Skillets, glasses, knives, dishes cover every counter. She has made twelve tomato pies. There's the wine, have some. Jane's clay sculptures, books, more books, squashed-down chairs where you really can read. Who's staying over? Always there's a guest or two and an unmade bed. Unobtrusively hanging over a chest, the painting of a woman; the signature of the artist makes your eyebrows rise. Really? This *is* a museum of sorts.

The long table she sets with unironed linen and gay abandon but with many candles. Flowers in small crystal vases and jelly jars. Generous platters make the rounds. Always on hand, a country ham. Have more. She saves the printed sacks they come in. By note or email, she has invited everyone. (She does not speak on the phone.) "Come for Billie Holiday's 'Summertime,' and low-country boil." At Christmas, she passes to us her collection of falling-apart black hymnals and we sing—loud, exaggerating *the stars are brightly shining. It is the night* . . . Crab time. Corn time. Truffle, peach, cherry. Grab the occasion and celebrate. The kitchen ferments with what's ripe now. From afar, walking through her house, I pause in the bathroom. It's crowded with baskets of towels, a stack of magazines, perfume bottles and lotions. Regulated to a wall at the corner by the sink, there's Jane as a young Virginia Woolf–type beauty in black and white. That far-past-you gaze and good bones. One of the Olympians.

Lee's big place sits way back from busy Churton Street on a raft of buttercups. Lee's big heart and mind. The old place was gussied up with trim during the Victorian era but underneath remains the four-square structure with the separate red-brick kitchen building still standing. We could be inside a house that's in one of her novels. We're almost always on the front porch or at the kitchen table, which is never without several vases of flowers, *The New York Review of Books,* a plate of pastries, the daily *New York Times*—still in the print version—and books read, yet to read, or to pass on. I will leave with at least two. Manuscripts from aspiring writers used to be stacked on the kitchen table, too. Now they're arriving digitally but still in droves. She will comment on every one. (It's rumored she's a saint.) Even the invasive will never know when they've intruded on her time. Four ladies in search of the antebellum Burwell School wandered in the front door and began chatting and looking around. Lee emerged from her writing trance and ended up giving them a tour of her own house, then tea. From Lee's upstairs study, her prodigious works emerge. The house cooperates. From the front yard, we watch the town Christmas parade. Rugs are spread and cookies passed around. And at her annual holiday party with two Christmas trees, the bar is set up in the hall, and a burgeoning number of guests pick at the pimiento cheese and biscuits and chicken skewers in the dining room. Once a stranger walked in thinking he was at another address, liked what he saw, stayed to party, and no one asked, Who are you? That kind of house.

Kate's house haunts me. Kate curled by the fire with her iPad. Warhol's Richard Nixon over the fireplace always grated. That was one thing I never understood, when her taste was for hand-woven rugs, folk art, antique textiles. Must have been that second husband. How could she look at a Nixon smirk every day? But we all loved the fall concert in that spare, elegant room with Cole Dalton playing the piano, and the hour after when we honored him, and the sweet occasion created by Kate. She and I had many secrets. How we laughed. Maybe we regretted some of them later. Kate's workroom, where she created Joseph Cornell–like dioramas at the expansive long table spread with her collages, poetry notebooks, sketched images. She was attracted to powerful men but had their number. She and I pored over the letters her father wrote home from World War II. He was a liberator of

Dachau. What to do with this stash of letters from a boy from Cameron, Missouri, who would return and take over the family cemetery monument business? Kate, her wispy beauty. Her Woodside house, essential California, which she, too, became. When cancer struck her spine, she was (outwardly) upbeat as always, baking brown butter plum tart, reading literary travel books, taking long walks with friends when she could. The family swirling around. When the time came, her bravery shocked me to my feet. Her decision is one no one should ever have to make. It came down to her, great lover of her life, in her glass and shiny wood haven, to raise the glass of water and swallow a pill. I'm imagining Kate at that moment, more alone in her home full of light than I can fathom. Even the decision: Where shall I lie down? There, on her daybed covered with kilims and pillows. Late-day slant of light bouncing off the glass walls from the western evening. The many windows overlooking her drought garden will not reflect her yoga poses.

Fred and Jimmy, Jimmy and Fred. Far in the country Fred and Jimmy live in two structures, a weathered board house where they sleep, and a repurposed barn where they work, cook, entertain. Private and public. On their land, they've built a pyramid thirty feet high of hog wire with a narrow opening to the interior. In summer, morning glories, gourds, and squash climb the wires, creating a green secret space where you sit inside on funky lawn chairs and have a glass of rosé and think you're in "Jack and the Beanstalk." Pergolas, a little pond, surprising beds full of specimen plants (meaning "What is that, Jimmy?"). In a dusty room adjacent to the barn, Fred keeps his three vintage Alfa Romeos, each in dif-

ferent stages of restoration. A succulent-lined wooden walkway leads into the studios and living space. Their bookcases
are arranged perpendicular to the wall like library stacks.
Around the perimeter, space is left for changing exhibits of
Jimmy's line drawings and Fred's paintings. Also in the dining room, the walls provide a moveable feast for artworks.
These glimpses tell a lot about who these two men are and
why they are alluring. But another thing—the summer dining
room. Left on the property, near the barn, stands a weathered-
to-a-sheen wooden tobacco-drying structure from another
era. About the size of a one-car garage, open on both sides,
the structure leans a bit. Racks at the top held the tobacco
leaves. It stands empty except when we have dinner there on
summer nights, a breeze off the pond blowing straight
through. They've set a raw board table with silver and lanterns and armfuls of wildflowers and weeds. Fireflies sail
through. Gazpacho, herb-crusted rack of lamb, little greens,
Atlantic Beach pie. The deep country sounds of tree frogs and
owls and something scary howling. Black night, our faces
around the table burnished in candlelight. This kind of night
brings out stories. At home in their home. Talk. Talk. Talk.

Ann's house—one of the oldest in Chapel Hill. Prim and
upright, facing historic Franklin Street, which should have
been protected from traffic but was not. All the lovely old
houses pounded by noise. You can imagine the former leafy
neighborhood of yore, gracious professors' homes, but now
most have become sororities and fraternities, who were allowed willy-nilly expansions so that Ann's house is the petu-
nia in the pumpkin patch. During fall rush, as we sit out on
the backyard patio sampling Ann and Randall's exquisite hors

d'oeuvres, we hear the Chi Omega (ah, my old sorority!) sisters chanting about how great they are. I'm sure they are. Randall, a trial lawyer, will bring up politics and soon we're raving, loud as the coeds. Ann grew up here, adored her grandfather, whose house this was. He is revered as an enlightened president of the University of North Carolina. There's the original sprigged wallpapers against which Ann has hung, above her grandmother's piano, an oversized photograph of an androgynous child in drifty white, and a dramatic shot of wildfires raging across California in the narrow hallway. There's a shot of a prisoner at Guantánamo and a portrait of Edna Lewis, one of Ann's idols. Who can explain the back sunporch furnished with tramp art—pyramidal squat table and floor lamps made from popsicle sticks, other tables from crates, and humpy cane furniture. A hanging lamp from pick-up sticks. At her oval dining table, Ann lights many votives. Because Ann is droll, a perfectionist, and likes to surprise, we sit down to eat what we've never tasted before, a little soup of radishes and curry, quail stuffed with pecans and herbs, long simmered in cognac, a tian of vegetables arranged like a mosaic. Monograms on vintage linen napkins rise like veins on the hands of Grandmother Stewart. And always flowers. Not roses or sunflowers but seductive ranunculus and anemones in julep cups. The past has been brought along, not sent to the attic. The grandparents, long interred, could join us for dinner.

Steven and Randy named their house It Had Wings after an Allan Gurganus (a neighbor) short story. When I saw the I-beam-shaped white board house, I thought the name meant that once the house had wings that perhaps had burned. Also,

its square-columned, small porch reminded me so much of
the house where I grew up that it seemed spooky. Is it spooky?
In a good way. These are two collectors—wait, maybe one
impassioned collector and one smiling enabler—whose ac-
quisitions overrun any idea of a normally furnished house.
Their obsession: architectural models of vernacular American structures. There was one, bought on a whim. Then a few
more. Now the holdings have caused the construction of
Georgian outbuildings—small temples—holding more and
more of the miniature meticulous churches, railroad stations,
hotels, residences, courthouses, stores—I don't think there's
a doghouse, but maybe. Hundreds. Some are lit and you
imagine the life within. Tiny furniture and organs and pews
and church bells. All need dusting from time to time. A few
feathers from the duster catch in shutters and chimneys.
Whimsy became world-class collection. They live there. The
cat steps gingerly over and around the thousand models, mi-
raculously not overturning. The real rooms squeeze in a
piano, a bed, a dining room table, a charming and cozy living
space albeit hemmed in by the darling structures and the walls
covered with oil paintings of, yes, early American houses. At
the constant parties, Randy steps back with his enigmatic
smile but Steven speaks up for all the celebrations in his ken.
Any artist visiting our town is feted (watch your elbows) and
welcomed with rhyming verses and toasts. Any local who has
published or displayed or acted, or just had a birthday, gathers
for champagne. Imagine the collection after midnight. Do the
inhabitants of the models resume a life? Steven and Randy are
dreaming. Is Randy dreaming of minimalist rooms while Steven fantasizes about finding an early model of the White

House? When they are gone, what becomes of this quirky and magnificent collection? Maybe it will be moved out into some rigid space where schoolchildren will be brought and lectured to about nineteenth- and twentieth-century architecture. For now, it's ours, friends of Steven and Randy.

Michael mourned Burnside, his old house where he could have string quartet concerts for fifty. The dining table extended to seat our intimate circle of twenty-five friends, aka the Revelers. The dreaded word *downsize* was thrown at him by his more practical wife, Maureen, who might have been tired of manning the giant mower, managing and performing constant repairs to the venerable property. We all hated the sale. The place was part of our psyches, too. Burnside centered our community. Auctions for charities and fundraisers for reasonable candidates were held on the lawn; in winter the doors opened to New Year's galas and poetry readings, even memorial services. New Yorkers moving south snapped it up. The grand piano was given to a local singer. The gate was closed for good. In the seven-block move, the family silver was lost. Soon Michael didn't have time to mourn. While he traveled with us and other friends to Puglia, Maureen announced by phone that she'd bought the King Street Tavern, an eighteenth-century watering hole near downtown. Long since converted to a residence, the house still needed massive work. But after, what a charmer for retirement. Lock and go. Focus and write. They transformed. Suppers in the low dining room ensued. A copper tub graced Michael's bath. A room under the eaves, now whimsically wallpapered in blue toile, looked like Jane Austen slept there. The odd slopes of the garden were revised to advantage, and further improve-

ments were planned. Maureen began to write a book in the
tiny English-style study, all prints and firedogs and a desk
under the window. She felt at home. Michael complained.
There was little space to entertain. He knew about himself but
knew it hard now. So that's home to him. Where one's friends
come. I was vaguely looking at houses for sale. When I saw
the wretched two-story colonial just up the street from them,
I called. "Let's go look. It has good bones." The widow Ray
had died, without ever updating since the 1950s. There was
everything to do—porch, windows, leaky sunroom, heat, air,
kitchen. But the double living room with gracious windows,
wide porch, numerous big square rooms, hinted at the expansive feel of Burnside. We stood there in the wreck envisioning
linen curtains billowing at the long windows, a snuggery with
deep chairs, and a wall of books. But no one was crazy. This
house required another round of devotion ever so much more
ardent than restoring their current house. One night after dessert at the Tavern, Michael looked up at the low ceiling,
poured a splash of wine, and said, "This house makes me feel
like I'm in a coffin." A silence fell around the table. *Home* was
not going to happen. After that, Maureen agreed that they
were brave enough for one more reno. So it began at the
widow Ray's. Two years in, there's still work to accomplish,
but the foyer is papered in red and black monkeys—how
bold. The huge plywood kitchen transformed first. We
gasped! Pink tile, begone. A new copper tub, the attic morphed
into a study. Maureen's birthday was just celebrated. Lanterns
along the still-rough porch, the long table set with new silver,
thanks to insurance. We were in Italy but heard the music.

If ever I could believe in elves and fairies, no kidding, it would be in the Tuscan chestnut forest where Susie and Rowan live. The massive trees spread into a canopy of gold in fall, green-lit in spring, and weighted dark shade in summer. Porcini mushrooms thrive, perhaps giving rise to the fantasy that fairies might shelter beneath them. Fiat-size stones rest where they tumbled a millennium ago, old gods churning up the earth. Skirting a ridge, you catch glimpses far below of the Val di Chiana spreading flat and verdant to the horizon. Yes, they are isolated up here. Miles from their friends in Cortona. Home was Melbourne but not now. They have visceral connections to their aerie. *I saw the house and I was home.* Sounds familiar to me. After you wind through the mythic forest, the white road ends at a long stone farmhouse with attached greenhouse room. Much of the action takes place in this light-lifted space. Usually, we are ten at table. The courses roll out, sometimes nostalgic curries, lamb, and Pavlovas. She even makes a delicious carrot cake, and I've never liked carrot cake. Rowan knows his vino and often blind pours, asking us to guess. He must often be disappointed as we flail and hold out the glass for more. These two sunny Aussie extroverts throw lavish picnics and luncheons that seem professionally catered and served, though there's no hired soul at all. Lunch will go on until five and there's the day gone. Up here above the olive line, you sense a bit of magic. What do friends do? Talk. After one dinner we shared, Susie wrote to me about the evening's conversation. We covered, she said, "From medical assessments to books (of course), faith, dishwasher-stacking, God, linen-folding, the meaning of Home and place, music, poetry and genius, introversion, COVID, musical theatre and West Side Story ('It's on in London! Let's go!'), beauty and Venice

('Let's go now! We'll be there by 1 A.M.!'), farting pigs and belching cows, San Marino ('The only region I haven't been to—let's go NOW! We could be there by 3 A.M.'), cliffs and beaches (a chorus of 'I want to live there, if I can't live here!'), hearts, other lives in San Francisco, Denmark, North Carolina, and Australia, passion, the Olympics, the superiority of dogs, the names we wanted to be called, Cortona's festivals and . . . The tune was lively, with many crescendos splitting the peace of the nearby *cinghiale*, wild boar. We loved it all." Everyone loves a circle of warmth and spontaneity. But back to the isolation. Here's the thing. Those friends, who spark such conversation and pleasure in their company, close the door behind us and retreat into profound solitude. They're gardening, reading, planning—what are they doing up there? Perhaps they're close to the huge stone fireplace, writing, telling stories exactly where *contadini* (farmers) used to sit recounting stories with vin santo to double warm them. Often no one sees them for days. They thrive inside their four walls. Why else select a house so far into never-never land?

At Susan's white brick house, open the yellow door and what's the aroma? Cardamom, cumin? Fenugreek? She wins for most coveted dinner invitation. Not wanting dark wood in her house, she painted an extendable Duncan Phyfe–style table with several coats of white. In the corner of the dining room, Scruffy, mongrel dog of the soulful eyes, attends all parties from his bed. He has at least fifty toys that he transports up and down the stairs. If hors d'oeuvres have been forgotten in the living room, he instantly scarfs up a plate of salumi or a bowl of nuts. In this house, guests are not allowed to help serve or clear. Susan does everything. Her mission:

She will feed you. Feed you so well. Why aren't Michelin stars handed out to home cooks? Always there are bouquets in the kitchen, on the dining room table, and on the round table by her kitchen window, where we plot what we will cook when and who will come. We have a cookbook project in the works and try to get the recipes organized and divvy up who's testing what. We exchange news. Samia is going to Egypt, Tom is having a knee replaced, Susan is raising funds for Afghan refugees. Have you seen the bodacious purple clematis in bloom on Hope Street? So much to say. We admire the pale aqua glassy tiles and the good cabinetwork from the recent remodel. For seven months, she cooked with a microwave at her desk upstairs and a gloom descended on the house during the kitchen exile. As if a tourniquet had tied off her creativity. I'm inspired by her ambitious duck confit, preserved lemons, cassoulet, and, she announces, she's about to go through the whole Turkish repertoire. Talented as she is in the kitchen, she has a poison thumb in the garden. Her patio pots languish, except for one curry plant that merits her attention. During lockdown, she continued to entertain, with all the gloves and wipe-downs and distancing we had to practice. Out of the dining room, with its Provençal checked clothes and pretty dishes, we marveled at what was served on paper plates at little tables outdoors. It seemed like dead geraniums were commenting on the situation we found ourselves in. But we had bright stars through the oaks. The talk was good, and Ed could always find the songs someone thought of and play them on his device. Often, we turned up "Goodbye to You" and sang it to the virus and the lax politicians and whatever had landed us outside the comforts of home. Fanciful, but from here in Italy, I can see Susan, all five burners ablaze, stirring the pistachios into the lemon cream for pasta. The table is set. I even know who's coming for dinner.

At Allan's, the jungle-fever ferns, canna lilies bright as roosters, and looming banana plants envelop you as you approach his yellow shingled and gabled early Victorian. On the wraparound porch, one literary luminary or another might be sipping wine and trying Allan's perennial shrimp plate. Drop-in neighbors are welcome, too. When you enter the foyer, the feeling is kaleidoscopic. Papered in a nostalgic William Morris willow-leaf pattern, the walls are covered in early-American reverse-painted mirrors. In this romantic, quirky house, Lewis Carroll or A. A. Milne could live, even Beatrix Potter, but instead of her pots of paint, stacks of books grow. Beside chairs, on tables, shelves, books everywhere. Where you might expect a vase of daffodils on the dining room table, ramous branches of dog rose entwine into the chandelier. Where you think a desk should be stretches a room-length surface piled with papers. Above, normal windows have been replaced with a reclaimed gothic church window. They overlook the Presbyterian cemetery of mossy stones and leaning obelisks and sunken gravestones. Like Allan's paraprosdokian sentences (the first half is disrupted by the last half), the syntax of the rooms is surprise. Coral walls, black-and-white floor, globes, sculptures, especially heads, masks. A maximalist resides here, and why would his prose be any different? Home, where there's freedom to invent, to subvert. Clear that someone pays no tax to Caesar. The house always has spirits but especially on Halloween when Allan and pals perform political morality plays for the innocent kiddies expecting miniature Snickers. A line forms all the way to the corner, and no child will forget that thrilling night in the haunted house when politicians rose from their coffins and repented.

It's difficult to track Elspeth because I don't know her home of the moment. Five years ago, children suddenly grown, Els and Clay began a vagabond existence. She stages luxury houses that are for sale. He's in real estate. (At this point, home may be three adjacent storage units filled with their furniture.) I've seen English engravings of eighteenth-century agricultural workers migrating to the next seasonal job. The moves were called "flitting," which makes it sound easy. Carts piled to teetering, even the children carrying pots and pans. Els stuffs her Suburban, calls a mover. They juggle sofas, headboards, paintings, picking from their stash what fits the next place. They've got it down. Pack, go, unpack, order in, style, live there until the house sells. Sometimes two months, sometimes six. We visit and feel like five-star guests. Then they relocate. They exemplify John Keats's Negative Capability—to be capable of "being in uncertainties" without always reaching for conclusions. A state open and ready. How long, I ask, until you feel at home? Els answered easily. Three days. By then the herbs and spices are in alphabetical order. Advantages: no clutter accumulates. They've left behind seventeen houses. Each was unmistakably Els's house. I may see her in the Georgian mansion, but she's moved on to Tudor or Tuscan or Provençal. They settle into one posh place after another, and another . . . Don't holidays blur? Don't you miss the one with the covered pergola and tiled pool? Don't you always have to have everything tidy? Yes, yes, and yes.

Margaret's home, like my other friends', could only belong to the owner. But more so. A former fishing camp, primitive and slapped together, became her eccentric perch on the Eno River. She and her friends gather to make things. Papier-mâché lanterns, quilts, costumes for the parades, or plum jams in the bright blue tile kitchen. Art structures from found materials. In the living room sits a vintage barber's chair. I said quirky, didn't I? Pretty stones and twisted pieces of wood. Most heavenly—a two-story screened porch where she can sleep upstairs on a pile of quilts, sequestered, as in a treehouse, with the musical falls of the river over rocks. Margaret loves the seclusion of the woods and all its snakes, turtles, skunks, foxes. She collects photos of initials and hearts that lovers have carved into bark around her forest. On walks, she spots the wild ginger, the hawk, what the owl coughed up. When the pond before her house floods her road, she can enter only via a raised catwalk. Then she's up on the rise where the cabin stays dry, and she's detached from the fray. Porches here and there, made for comfort. She's on her own terms. What a solace from her job of exposing sex trafficking, and writing grants for agencies to fight it, giving seminars to awaken organizations to the breadth of that evil. There's the path to the river, where she also can lie out in the sun naked on big flat boulders. Or fish or wade. The river is the architect of the house.

At Francesca's cottage on the edge of the woods, a screen is set up on the deck. On benches and makeshift chairs, we'll be watching De Sica movies tonight. Maybe *Bicycle Thieves* or *Marriage Italian Style*. (Please, not the horrific *Two Women*.) Her home does not reflect her. Vivid she is; the house remains a neutral backdrop, a place to perch, ready to fly. There is a cat. There is a vegetable plot. But Francesca is on the move, designing stage sets, traveling to Argentina to tango, losing herself in her memoir of her outrageous Italian ancestors. During Covid lockdowns, she devised an odd quest: daytrips to visit all the county courthouses in North Carolina. Francesca casts her bread upon the waters. Her house says, *I don't have to live here.* She may reside permanently in the States, but I see her most clearly in the villas and farms in the country of her birth. As if this life has detached from the real and is spinning a new orbit. We friends love the exploits of the talented, larger-then-life, difficult Italian family she comes from. There has been much to forgive, and she has accomplished that. An American cottage is the last place one would imagine she would settle. But here she is, among us. She's designing toys and a complex puzzle, probably googling flight departures to FCO. When the film starts, the house disappears. Popcorn, owl calls, wine, flickering light.

Jean's dining room window frames a classic view of the Tuscan hills, vineyards, the noble profile of Cortona in the distance. You could be standing in that spot for hundreds of years and nothing would have changed. Is this the most peaceful landscape in the world? Along a kitchen counter, maybe one hundred identical jars line the wall. They hold every bean, spice, grain, herb known. Any old *nonna* can set to cooking right here. The restoration shows impeccably the volumes of the structure, untainted by competing messages to the eye. The rest of the house is starkly, elegantly minimalist, almost anonymous. Black-and-white photographs identically framed. White sofas. Glass, spare white rooms, the plaster smooth as

boiled frosting. She and Aziz are not tempted by the local antiques and paintings, or the colorful majolica. The plates are
white. Open a kitchen drawer to be dazzled by the surgical
layout of the whisk, knives, and spatulas. There's the creeping
feeling that these worldly, funny, acerbic people might just be
more evolved than you are. While most of us in old houses
have our clothes jammed into *armadios*, they turned a narrow
room into that rare local commodity, a closet. We're getting a
little private here, so just to say, I imagine a queen's wardrobe
could aspire to be this orderly. No shoe has a crust of dirt. No
dry cleaner hangers and plastic allowed here. It's all serene
and they are not especially serene people. There's usually a
drama unfolding. There's the key. As Wallace Stevens wrote:

> *The house was quiet because it had to be*
> *The quiet was part of the meaning . . .*

Coco lavishes her considerable energies on her Tuscan
house. She's situated just below Le Celle, the ancient monastery where Saint Francis spent a winter and where a few Ca-
puchins remain. They stride along the road like kindly spirits,
white hair flying, sometimes barefooted. They, the ones
whose brown robes and white trim gave cappuccino its name.
There's a holy aura to the densely wooded surroundings.
Maybe the bells resonating across the hills, maybe the great
rush and fall of spring water before the stacked golden bee-
hive of the great edifice, maybe the Stations of the Cross walk
that threads up the terraced land. Coco's house falls under
that benevolent aegis. It even has a stark small chapel with a
consecrated altar. What luck—few interior designers get to

restore chapel interiors. At the Arezzo antiques market, Coco
found suitably austere chairs and religious statues and paintings. Not especially religious, she and Jim just thought the
house required this respect. Their pale stone villa rests on a
plinth of arbored roses and mounds of hydrangeas, with lavender paths leading into the hills. She and I share the house
obsession. Our texts focus on desks, colors, tiles, fabrics, who
can rewire, who can build a table base, and what the hell was
Carlo thinking when he used that grout that looks like bubble
gum, when he *knew* . . . There's a line to cross when you're
putting together a house. You furnish to your liking and comfort. It's done. Home. Guests will enjoy visiting in the big
rooms overlooking the Val di Chiana. The kitchen cabinets
are exactly the right cobalt blue. Cross the line and you're in
another realm. Coco and I long since passed into that golden
zone. ("You must sweeten the house a little bit every day," my
sister once advised.) Does the ever-evolving desire for beauty
at home derive from a super sense of conviviality? Coco often
meets tourists in town while having coffee in the piazza. Soon,
that Indian eyewear designer will be invited to lunch and will
always remember the linens, the friendly chats, the fried zucchini flowers, the cold cucumber soup, and the peach tart.
Coco's long table, set with bowls of green hydrangeas, forms
part of all the local expats' summer memories, and in fall, the
olive oil tasting on the night we've pressed our olives, big
cheer, big wines, and chestnuts in the coals. But let's not even
pretend the obsession is all about welcoming friends. We
would be hounding the antiques markets even if no guest ever
came. We'll always wander into the study at midnight and
start rearranging the bookcase, if not rearranging the furni-

ture. We are engaged in a long personal dialogue with four walls. How to tweak this room to make it interest me more, how to go to the next level with colors now that the dead pine no longer blocks the light? Enlarge the small bathroom, re-cover the faded chairs, replace, repaint, replant. It's constant, this outer manifestation of an inner drive. From the precipi-tous hillside, way in the distance, the lights of the train whether you are there or not slip across the landscape, bring-ing someone near, taking someone away.

THE TASTE OF MEMORY

With my whole body I taste these peaches.

—WALLACE STEVENS,
"A DISH OF PEACHES IN RUSSIA"

A SAN FRANCISCO FRIEND TOLD ME HIS IDEAL OF DOWN-home cooking is pan-fried sand dabs. Around Chapel Hill, people flock to Mama Dips for nostalgic fried chicken. And if not there, to one of the many barbecue places around the Triangle. Barbecue is almost a religion. My Minnesota-raised husband recalls his mother's pot roast but longs most for the creamy graham cracker pie he and his brother would steal and run upstairs to devour. Anytime he gets together with his sisters, that pie is on the table. I might think, *Nice, but what's the big deal?* But then I remember that the food of home becomes mythic through memory.

Growing up in Georgia, we lived close to the land. We cooked what was raised locally and did not know the foods of other cultures that we now enjoy. Chinese, Japanese, Mexican, Italian were from other stratospheres. I knew the story of okra seeds and peanuts sewn into the hems of women's skirts before they were forced onto the slave trade ships. I was taught, too, how the Native Americans ground corn and cooked it in the coals, along with grilled meat. Georgia cracker and Black farm cooking centered around greens, corn, and pork. We knew the layering of heritage English and German desserts, dishes such as aspics, pressed chicken, towering cakes, rolls, biscuits. All of this blended into our rural cuisine. Everyone, rich or poor, ate hog jowl, fatback, cornbread, black-eyed peas with rice and chopped scallions (the nostalgic Hoppin' John), cane syrup, cracklins, chitlins, bacon, hush puppies, goober peas (peanuts) boiled in the shells, collards, turnips, and pole beans. We know many of these now as "soul food." The apt name became famous with the migration of Black people taking their favorite foods with them out of the South.

For all, it was *See what you've got and get on with it*. In the South that would include alligator, fern fronds, ramps, rattlesnake, turtle, squirrel, opossum, and the unforgettable cold 'coon and collards.

The term *soul food* was appropriated, like other aspects of Black culture. Maybe because English lacks a word for describing how I feel when I want to talk about ham biscuits and pecan pie. But all over the world, we find terms for food evocative of home. My Danish friends Mikael and Jan refer to *livret*, a word I wish we had. Life-dish. Perfect. A special dish you cherish all your life. A taste reminds you of times past, of your family's kitchen, maybe something your grandmother would make and no one ever could come close. When Jan served his mother's cloudlike lemon dessert, I understood instantly. Suvir, a chef and friend in Delhi, tells me about *ghar kaa khaana*, recipes loved and most respected in a home. Ask friends what they remember as "life-dishes" and hear a recital of foods that take them home. Even if home has been a moving proposition.

From our years in San Francisco, we still taste Julia Child's cheese soufflé. We used to whip one up once a week, especially after we got a new stove and the puffy soufflé scraped the top of the oven. A default choice, especially with crisp Little Gem lettuces from the farmers' market. This was a giant step for me because when I lived alone and got home late from work, I often spent dinnertime on my small balcony overlooking the lights of the city, eating ice cream from the carton with a fork. Not the Country Captain Chicken of my childhood, but, still, soufflés and Cherry Garcia ice cream became my down-home food because memory is a moveable feast.

THE EXPERIENCE OF A loved dish can reach far back and pull forward memories of when and where you casually leaned over the bowl for a whiff of homemade vegetable soup. But memory is rarely just of food. The soup in the green bowl was always served by my favorite aunt when I went to visit in Vidalia. At her place, I escaped my disruptive family and could be a child, not a mini-adult trying to negotiate peace. She set a bountiful table, as generous as she was. Food memories are sharp and loaded because food triggers remembering who and where you were when you ate "a plate full of Jerk Chicken and rice, sitting on a white sandy beach under a palm tree with a cold bottle of beer," as my friend Jean remembers, "a lot of Bob Marley playing in the background."

I asked several friends—what's your most memorable

food from home? What comforts, revives, and provokes memories? Susie, an Australian with Italian affinities, wrote back:

> A piece of thickly buttered toast, whose melting butter you lick from your fingers, the familiar scent of Mum's Afghan biscuits, the smell wafting and lingering around the kitchen. A hearty pumpkin soup that runs down your chin as you dunk torn chunks of bread into it. My comfort food is a steaming square of lasagna, filling and warming your heart like a Roberta Flack song. Also, sitting in front of an open fire cooking a crumpet, drizzling it with honey and eating it greedily. Crunching on thick nutty chocolate so that your mouth becomes glued, and you can't possibly speak.
>
> Comfort food is a memory left over on the table, accompanied by the squeak of your chair, the clattering of spoons, a smattering of conversation, the laughter of friends, steam rising from plates, the sound of the doorbell, the warm buzz of family and the sharing of smiles and looks and stories. This food warms, fills, and nurtures, while recognizing that you have been there before, and the feeling of it is like re-catching a dream.

"Like re-catching a dream."
Yes, exactly. A riveting response. Wonder what Afghan biscuits are. I should have foreseen what a laden question I'd asked.

"Meat pies at the Footie with Dad and my brothers . . . and our team always won. Sandwiches at the 'G,' watching the Aussies play the mighty bowlers from the West Indies . . . where we didn't always win. Awful pies and peas at the Uni café while learning the law. Fish and chips by the sea after a great day at the beach." So wrote Rowan: soul-catcher memories tied to place.

From Seattle, Sheryl recalled:

A glass of Prosecco on the bench at Il San Pietro while watching the sun go down over the pink cliffs of Positano. A steaming plate of bucatini *cacio e pepe* from 13 Gobbi in Montefollonico. Popcorn floating in butter with lots of salt, with a glass of red wine while watching *Il Postino*. Homemade rye bread baked by my Finnish grandmother, just pulled from the wood-burning oven and smothered with sour cream and lox.

More from Jean:

After a long, hard day sailing in Cornwall with friends, pulling into The Pandora for fresh pasties scoffed from a greasy bag, leaning against the bar and sharing near misses in our charge to win the race. Mother's rice pudding made with our Guernsey cow's milk wasn't bad either. It had to have a dollop of clotted cream on top and a spoonful of strawberry jam added. That put hairs on your chest.

Jane wrote to me from her enchanted house in the woods:

Down-home food tells me not who but what I am
and right now I am a creature knowing corn bread.
For me, this food is almost always either old, long-
remembered, and long-wanted food, very particular,
or things right out of the garden very little inter-
fered with. The look and taste of loved food regis-
ters as emotion. In this way, cooking becomes a way
of instinctual, immediate communication, happily
without need of words. Sharing food can be a kind
of intimacy. I almost always cook food that takes me
back.

As a child in a peripatetic military family, Coco's memories roam the world:

Okinawa, Japan, Austria, Italy, and finally the USA,
where I discovered and loved Coke machines and club
sandwiches. At five in Austria, housing was at an inn,
where my sister and I had the same breakfast every
day: hot chocolate and thinly rolled buttered pancakes
filled with jam. Stationed in Italy, the food imprinted
indelibly. I was introduced to spinach lasagne, salumi,
gelato, tomato sauce, and many tastes that never
left me.

She writes that she was "a skinny little girl running all
over Livorno" gathering cheeses, bread, olives. She credits
those tastes to her ending up with a home in Italy, where she

has a mighty stove and is famous locally for her plum and peach tarts.

Her husband Jim / Giacomo, with 100 percent Italian roots via New Jersey, didn't write but told me that pasta with his mother's "gravy" (tomato-based ragù) takes him to Sunday at home. Pasta, pasta, pasta drying on sheets in the kitchen, ravioli formed and poached lightly, so many pastas. Masterful as she was at making pasta, his mama's much-loved ricotta cheesecake hid a secret, and it was not the drops of rosewater or the candied lemon peel. The recipe she left behind described forming little balls of pie crust, rolling them into small circles, and patching them in the pan. Turns out, she couldn't roll out a pie crust in one piece. Afternoons in the kitchen, where he and his mother sat together for tea with biscotti to dip, engendered a lifelong habit of four o'clock teatime, always with a biscuit and a memory or two.

THE APERTURE WIDENS. The strongest food passions are real but also symbolic, a moving cloud of memory and taste. It's not just the coconut cake, it's the scene of my mother carrying it into the dining room. The graham cracker pie two brothers stole from the kitchen was their rebellion and bond, relished long after the crumbs on the bedspread. My friends and I in high school raiding a watermelon field at night counted as adventure in a place where there wasn't much going on. Is that why I still love watermelon above all fruits?

I used to teach the "objective correlative" in poetry classes. T. S. Eliot, in his essay "Hamlet and His Problems," wrote about the writer needing to find the particular image that works to convey the heft of the emotion the writer wants to express. "Do I dare to eat a peach / I shall wear white flannel trousers and walk upon the beach," and the drippy peach and the stainable trousers deliver the speaker's tentative approach to life. As would my broken-open watermelon in a moonlit field, laughing friends, a farmer raising his overalls, flipping on the porch light, and reaching for his gun. . . .

Childhood food that proclaimed home shifted as I settled in different places. Outside my sunny California kitchen grew Meyer lemons and oranges. Avocados were plentiful, and guacamole by the pool with carafes of white wine and hot grapes merge in memory with literary readings and my daughter cartwheeling into the water. A summer in San Miguel taught me about the corn fungus huitlacoche, the slap of tortillas, and the spicy peppers women sold from their blankets at the *jardín* market. I'd come home (my home on Benito Juarez Park for three months) with bags of serranos, jalapeños, poblanos, and armfuls of heady-sweet tuberoses, the scents forever intertwined.

For an assault of food sensations, nothing compares with moving to Tuscany. Not just me, my whole family's idea of significant food shifted as we fell in love with what Fiorella, Placido, Giusi, Silvia, Gilda, Ivan, and Domenica—and their friends—were preparing to serve, the revelation of Italian *cibo casereccio*, home cooking. And what Riccardo, Claire, Fulvio, and Vittorio were pouring. The more I cooked, the more we pulled up our chairs to a lively *tavola*, indelible memories began to form around tortellini in *brodo*, rabbit simmered in *vin santo*, broccoli Romano, truffles, smoky pasta, the heady pork roast *porchetta*, on and on.

When our grandson came home after a year of studying in Shanghai, we asked what he most wanted to eat. Cheeseburgers, burrito, roast chicken, steak? No. He asked for spaghetti *al ragù*. Out came the huge blue Le Creuset where we've cooked ragù a thousand times. When his plane landed, the rich aromas already suffused the kitchen, and Rocco, Will's labradoodle, hung around the stove, excited that Will was coming home or maybe just anticipating some leftovers.

No matter where we are, a pot of ragù often sits on the back burner. Because we invested in the hugest pot, we make a gargantuan triple recipe and freeze portions to mete out over the weeks of arriving home late, or spontaneously inviting someone to stay for supper. It's great with fusilli or rigatoni, but why bother? The classic is plain spaghetti, number 5. Other types of ragù—duck, *cinghiale* (boar), goose—exist, but in the hearts of Tuscans, nothing rivals the ubiquitous beef, pork, and sausage version. The secret—the long simmer.

. . .

Ragù

4 tablespoons extra-virgin olive oil

1 pound lean ground beef

1 pound ground pork

2 Italian sausages, casings removed

1 teaspoon salt

1 teaspoon black pepper

2 teaspoons fresh thyme

1 Mediterranean bay leaf
1½ cups red wine
1 cup mixed parsley, celery, carrot, onion,
    finely chopped
2 tablespoons tomato paste
16–20 fresh, ripe tomatoes or 2 28-ounce cans
    of tomatoes, chopped
Parmigiano Reggiano, grated

- Heat the olive oil in a heavy four-quart pot with a lid. Over medium heat brown all the meats, breaking up the sausages with a wooden spoon.
- After the meat browns, about ten minutes, add the salt, pepper, thyme, and bay leaf.
- Stir the red wine into the meat and simmer for about five minutes.
- Add the *soffritto* of parsley, celery, carrot, and onion, and the tomato paste and tomatoes.
- Bring the sauce to a boil, then lower to a calm simmer, cover, and cook for three hours, stirring now and then. Add a little more wine if you think the sauce is too dense. Parmigiano Reggiano, of course, of course, tops spaghetti *al ragù*.
- Spaghetti: Easy. When the big pot of water boils, add two tablespoons of table salt, the pasta, and cook for the time suggested on the package, usually eight to ten minutes. Test a couple of minutes early to see if it's done to your liking. *Al dente*, "to the tooth," means that the pasta is still a bit firm but not hard.

NOTE: *Soffritto,* from *soffriggere,* to cook at below-frying temperature, is the little handful of *odori* (smells)—parsley, celery, carrot, onion, and maybe basil—that the greengrocer stuffs in your bag. Finely chopped like French mirepoix, it's a base for much Italian cooking. Sauté it for six to eight minutes in some olive oil, though for the ragù, I skip the sauté, since it will be simmered for a long time. For other purposes, onion is added and, if you want, garlic. Make a big batch and use it in tomato sauce, or with bread crumbs to stuff tomatoes and zucchini, or to add to eggplant recipes.

These treasures, too, are hot-wired to sensations of home:

Caprese

This ubiquitous salad can be awful or sublime. It's all in the ingredients. Primo tomatoes thickly sliced, topped with creamy slabs of whole milk, fresh mozzarella, basil, salt, pepper, and a generous drizzle of top olive oil make this summer salad divine. Cut the quality of any one ingredient and it goes to so-so; cut two and we're down to wretched. Several days a week in summer, lunch outside overlooking the hills is caprese and slices of focaccia fresh from the local forno.

We don't drink wine at lunch, but a glass of chilled vermentino often comes to mind.

Melons

Cantaloupe was my mother's favorite food. On summer mornings, a pickup truck from the country stopped in our driveway and she flew out the door. Something about examining the stem end told her which was perfectly ripe.

I've tried growing cantaloupe in North Carolina, because for grocery stores, they're picked too early and no longer have the vine-ripe, heavenly fragrance they once had. Sugar sets when picked, true for many fruits. In my garden, when melons got close to ripeness some creature scaled the fence and took a chomp from each.

Here in Italy, Roberto at the *frutta e verdure* asks, "For today or tomorrow?" and judges several before he chooses. The cantaloupe skin is patterned like *rete*, "caul," webby and lacy. He holds up his selection, "From Cantalupo once upon a time." This I know because he's told me before. Someday I'd like to go to this village in Lazio named "Wolf Song," where Armenians coming to the papal court once brought seeds.

Every day from mid-June to the end of September I wake up to a bowl of cantaloupe on the kitchen counter. Ed, up earlier, trims the rinds and cuts the fruit into crescents. He's the cappuccino foam master, too; creamy, not frothy. I sit at our outside table, taking in the colors and clouds, with a book and a notebook. Some of the smeary clouds are the soft coral color of the cantaloupe.

Pici al'aglio

Antonello, our electrician, taught me a great *trucco* with pasta *al'aglio,* the simplest and one of the most loved pastas. When he gets home at ten after tracking underground wires in the dark, simple is best. You've got pasta and garlic and olive oil— good to go. Garlic is strong here. Eight cloves suffice for four nice servings. Traditionally, put the water on to boil, sauté a handful of minced garlic in ample olive oil, add salt and pepper, cook until soft over a low flame, then with tongs grab the dripping pasta and mix. If a bit dry, add some (about ¼ cup) of the starchy pasta water. Mix with grated Parmigiano and dinner's ready. Antonello taught me to chop the garlic, mince really, and— here's his secret—sauté only half, letting it almost brown. Add the cooked pasta, and then add the raw garlic. He brightens the taste with this little trick. I didn't mention to him that I sometimes add a squeeze of lemon juice, as that would be heresy. Some cooks add about a cup of tomato *passata* and some white wine but that seems like another thing altogether. Pici, a thick spaghetti, is a local favorite, but regular spaghetti is just fine.

The local Val di Chiana version of this recipe—pasta *al'aglione*—uses the milder fist-size garlic. In the States, the slightly smaller elephant garlic works. When I use that type, I chop three or four cloves, depending on the size, or about a cupful.

ALL THE CLASSIC EASY pastas of Italy, *cacio e pepe*, *arrabbiata* (hot, angry), tomato sauce, *al fumo* (smoky), share one attribute: They're more than the sum of their parts. Sit down with a steaming plate of any one of them and you're joining an ancient camaraderie of hungry people who had little to choose from, or little time to cook, or just appreciated the simple joys of eating.

Fagiolini del Lago Trasimeno

Summer's end brings tiny peas grown around the lake we can see from our house. They're a small crop, hard to grow, hand harvested. They must boil then simmer in a lot of lightly salted water. I toss in a couple of slices of *guanciale*, my substitute for the fatback we used in the South. Drain, but not totally, and dress with olive oil and salt.

Beige, with a tiny black dot, the peas are prized because they disappeared for hundreds of years until the 1960s, when they were rescued from oblivion. The earliest mentions are traced to the Etruscans. Did someone studying the tomb paintings spot a pot of these peas in scenes of the dead feasting and dancing? The peas are mentioned in a Greek plant history from 300 B.C. I like the fascinating origins, but they be-

came comfort food for me because they remind me of what
we called lady peas when I was small and had to shell them
into a colander on the back steps. My family adored delicate
but earthy lady peas. My mother paused the car and called out
to Mr. Bernhardt at the vegetable stand, "Are the lady peas in
yet?" If he shook his head, she'd speed off, saying, "You save
me some, you hear?" I call my sister in Atlanta. "Can you get
lady peas?" But she says no. Maybe millennia hence someone
there will revive them.

Zolfini

> The rare *zolfini*, another ancient legume I crave,
> grows only in the Casentino area above Arezzo.
> Flaxen and rounded, the pea is also delicate like its
> Trasimeno neighbor but incredibly buttery. Both
> of these special peas make great bruschetta and
> soups. If you travel to Tuscany, look for a packet
> of the dried peas and the *zolfini*. (There are online
> sources as well.)

Agretti

> Also called *la barba di frate*, friar's beard, this
> acidic vegetable looks like grass that grows under-
> water, and it tastes green. It kind of makes your
> teeth itch but in a good way. That's because it's
> full of minerals and properties that gladden the
> liver and whatever ails you. I don't love it because

of that. I'm just a fan of spring's bitter greens, such as rape, pronounced "rahp' a" (aka *pulezze*), broccolini (sometimes inexplicably called turnip tops), chicory, and pungent *puntarella*, chicory's wilder cousin, prized in the south of Italy. Our friend Mario, who owns the local restaurant Canta Napoli, drives all the way to Naples for his adored *puntarella*.

Ed likes to order a green for a first course—rape, spinach, *cicoria* or chard—when the delights of *agretti* or *puntarella* aren't available. *Agretti* translates to "saltwort" in English, but who ever heard of saltwort? It's kind of crunchy, has a piquant hit, but mostly I grab it as a sign of spring, emerald green, unique.

Chestnuts, Funghi Porcini

These two harbingers of fall fully represent Keats's opening to his ode "To Autumn": "Season of mists and mellow fruitfulness . . ." For a dozen years, we owned a stone house in a chestnut forest in the mountains above Cortona. I know no more exquisite pleasure than an October afternoon among those fabulistic trees, limbs light with golden leaves and the sun piercing through. The nuts already have fallen. Spiny shells lay open, resembling tiny hedgehogs, and within, the lustrous nuts. Our chestnut forest does not have the cathedral aura of the redwoods in California, but we see

a veiled golden sifting, a human scale that seems to
include the wanderer in an otherworldly aura. Just
find a log and listen to the silence. In these woods,
I picked baskets full of the big, prized *marrone*
kind. I learned to cut the X and roast them in the
fireplace. (Careful, they're loaded with calories.)

I took to adding them to my aunt Mary's turkey dressing,
spicing up the old Georgia recipe with a touch of Tuscany.
Boil a potful in full-bodied red wine and let them steep. Serve
with roasts, chicken, and especially duck confit.

NOW THE POETIC MOUNTAIN HOUSE, my favorite-ever house,
is sold, wedged into memory. I have never driven by to see it
and will not. But the chestnuts always take me there.

About *funghi porcini,* the most coveted Tuscan mushroom,
there is much to say, some of it not good. I have spent afternoons in the woods cruising for the elusive fungus. Two
sunny weeks after a good rain, they're found under oaks and
in secret places that hunters claim as their territory.

BATTERED AND FRIED PORCINI can't be beaten as an antipasto to serve with a cold glass of Franciacorta. Pasta with
sautéed mushrooms, parsley, and cream remain a standby.
I love to take home to the States cellophane packs of dried
mushrooms to soak in wine and use all winter. But once I was
at my neighbor's when she was cleaning mushrooms and I
saw her bring one close to her eyes. "What's that?" I asked.

"Oh, just worms." Just worms? At a fine restaurant in Bologna, I ordered the classic raw mushroom salad with slivered Parmigiano. Even in the dim light I saw wiggling on my plate. When I pointed out the worms to the waiter, he shrugged with no apology, much less the yelp I thought it merited. So . . . very fresh, very new. Otherwise, you might have unexpected company. I'm squeamish. (Would never try that mezcal with the ugly worm in the bottle.)

They are delicious, the mushrooms, that is. Why they became a favorite lies in the gathering. Roaming the damp woods, rustling through the leaves, imagining dryads slipping among the trees, the sweet fall air, the coming of the feasting season.

Turkey Breast, Rolled and Filled

> Until recently, home ovens were small in rural
> Italy. Baking has always been left to the town
> forno, or the outdoor bread oven, while meats are
> best cooked over real fire. The first fall I spent
> here, I planned to roast a turkey for Thanksgiving
> and invite stray Americans for the feast. In the
> butcher's window I saw the biggest turkeys I'd
> ever seen. They were the diameter of car tires. No
> way I could shove one of those giants into my
> oven. Enter the turkey breast, which now I prefer
> over all versions of the Thanksgiving bird.

Where I grew up, Fitzgerald played football against Tifton on Thanksgiving Day at two in the afternoon. Our fine browned bird was brought to the table at noon, the anticipation of its moist and tender slices mixing with the excitement of soon witnessing the Purple Hurricanes whip the Tifton Blue Devils. My new preference misses out on that nostalgic frisson but compensates with a more complex flavor. Gilda taught me to open a two-to-three-pound breast with zigzag cuts, then flatten it. Season with salt and pepper. Mix half a pound of ground veal with some bread crumbs, pistachios, thyme, more salt and pepper, and a splash of white wine. Spread the meat over the turkey. At this point, Gilda adds two peeled boiled eggs. Roll and tie, stripe with a few slices of pancetta. Roast, uncovered, at 350 degrees for half an hour per pound. During the last half hour, douse with a cup more of wine. Serve warm or at room temperature. The cross sections of boiled eggs make the slices pretty. Spoon on the pan juices. Say what you're thankful for.

FROM THE TERRACE EXTENDING from our kitchen, we consider the view as part of the meal. The hills unroll, undulate into valleys with pleats of green shadows and earth-colored farmhouses from time immemorial. From far windows, isolated squares of light glimmer. Who lives there? Who's bringing the pork roast to the table, who's pouring the wine Mirko made? Who's not coming home tonight? Who's the guest? Who's setting the table, who's mad? What are they talking about, who has a secret? What's to emerge tonight from the kitchen?

VI

RHYMES
WITH HOME

CHANGING THE
CHANGES

In HILLSBOROUGH, AS EVERYWHERE, FEAR OF COVID STRUCK a panic in minds as well as bodies. Not until later did I identify my urges with a trend: An avalanche of people decided to move. We were feverish, like the seventeenth-century Dutch willing to pay the price of a house for a tulip bulb. Moving offered an illusion of control, and the housing market went mad. Trapped by Covid, everyone scrambled to take charge or to pursue a delayed dream. Along with hordes of others, I felt gripped by the idea of change. Why? No doubt to be sorted out by future social analysts, but to me, it seemed that when our lives were threatened, the ground beneath our feet started to shake, too. Escape, some primitive force tells us. Seek higher ground. Anywhere but here. Instincts were stirred—or so it feels in hindsight. At the time, we told ourselves a different story.

I sometimes found waving on Chatwood's fence posts whole, transparent snakeskins. The snake snags onto a splinter and slowly slithers out, leaving behind a ghostly sleeve that once covered the sinewy body. I never saw a just-emerged snake, but I may know the sensation. Frustrated with feeling trapped at home, I began to clear the barn, attic, closets, to give away duplicate kitchenware and clothes. "Why *this* revision?" Ed asked. "Don't you have writing to revise?"

"I don't know. I just want a clean slate."

"There's no such thing. Clean slate is just a cliché."

Ed spends hours a day on the land. He always has taken in stride the wayward irrigation geysers, pumps that won't turn off, a skunk trapped under the house, a dryer that won't dry, a peeling rose arbor (didn't we just have that painted?). Then the normal maintenance issues that quadruple in a place like Chatwood began to turn on him. "Could you see about why the stream is clogged?" he asks plaintively. Surely, slowly, overtaking his enchantment with the land: the desire to be free. I sort manuscripts and defunct wills and fail once again to throw out letters from my college roommates. My daughter and I riffle through boxes of photographs, ditching only those of people we seemed fond of in the images but no longer remember.

But in the evenings, we sit on the front porch as many generations before us have done. The soft rain throws an aurous skein over the trees along the road. Ed brings out a pitcher of our favored drink, made from blackberry syrup, tonic, mint, a curl of orange peel. I practice my owl call, thrilled at the answering hoots. When one answers, I begin a conversation that must be baffling to the owl. If Ed has managed to write a poem, he reads it to me, and I tell him it's a work of genius. It is. We read aloud. Rilke. Sebald. We see the wet light fall across the stubbled field and the sky streak teal and pink behind the pines. The Annabelle hydrangeas bend their baby faces under the rain. Our two cats join us, as if we needed another reminder of how seductively beautiful this place is. We'd be fools to leave. And from nowhere expected: "The root of *husband*," Ed reminds me, "means 'housebound.'"

I've never wanted to travel more. That old saw: The only thing permanent is change.

Well into dark, we're talking travel. Turkey. Remembering travel. Portugal. With Covid we are not welcome anywhere. "Stay or go," I call out to the echo. And faintly from the trees I hear my last word, *gooooo* . . .

At least Chatwood is a world unto itself, if a demanding one. Extraction would be wrenching. But is there somewhere out there a solution that leaves us lighter?

After many front porch evenings, we surprise ourselves by deciding to sell these pleasing acres and rich rooms we've loved for a dozen years. Spend more time writing and living longer periods in Italy. Less on well filters, squirrel damage in the barn, fence repair . . .

We expected to wait a year, two, to sell a property like this. We shifted into high gear—the sprucing up of the outbuildings, professional photos, the write-up of Chatwood's history, the drone footage—all a waste of time. One call, one ad, the place sells the first day and we are reeling. Have we really done this?

I kept thinking of the Masaccio painting *Expulsion from the Garden of Eden*. Walking out of the garden of Eden, Adam and Eve look very sorry. Too late. We move into a low brick ranch in the Hillsborough historic district and become renters. Most furniture and books go into storage. The rooms are small. I like them. The retro kitchen wallpaper shows seed packets of herbs. The refrigerator is ominously black. The big square backyard adjoining others without fences reminds me of my first home, where we ran free across the neighborhood. It's September. Will we be here in spring to see the azaleas banking the house in bloom? One neighbor brings over Hoppin' John, another a pound cake. Honey. Flowers. We are living among people who leave cookies on the back porch. Shady walks become my new habit. It's nice—a real neighborhood after our isolated farm. There are towering trees I say hello to on my walks, a house where puppies are sheltered, always a pen of pure cuteness to visit, a cemetery where I find a tomb engraved MAYES, and another grave of a man, dead at twenty-three, called Crazy. His epitaph reads *Born to Lose,* and below it a carved marijuana leaf. In the Episcopal Church of Saint Mary, light piercing through stained glass colors the dark pews emerald and claret. For a moment I wish that I'd not fallen away from the church. I am astounded that we have sprung ourselves from the house we thought we'd live in forever. We feel that we've survived an accident or someone has died and this is the aftermath.

"WOULD YOU LIVE THERE? THERE?" I ask Ed. We take long drives. Deep country cottages lure but have no internet. We relax into village life quite easily. Our cat Fitz, peaceful angel, goes over to sit in my neighbor Joe's lap when he's in his glider. But Fitz also terrorizes a kitten who lives behind us, managing to open a screen porch door, steal toys and food, and cuff the kitten. Its owner knocks on the door. Polite, she asks if the marauder Fitz can be kept inside from three to five so her Poncy can play without the scary breaking and entering. As I'm totally in the wrong, I don't ask why she can't latch the door.

The virus rages and we travel nowhere. Days waste away as we scour real estate websites. Houses are snatched the moment listed. I see that it's even worse in other places, with people lined up to get a glimpse before they must make an outrageous bid or start over. We would love to stay in the homey neighborhood, but nothing comes up. In all of Hillsborough, nothing. We make an offer on a house just outside town, a wild price way over the asking, and are shocked that someone bid more.

After eight months in the sturdy house we call Three Little Pigs, we find another house. Though only fifteen years old, it looks like an overgrown barn in a wheat field crossed with an American suburban trophy house. Except for our bedroom and the sunroom, Chatwood was dark, the sacred old paneling too valued to paint. This place rife with sunlight seems right.

When I moved to North Carolina, I was featured in a newspaper. From the article, relatives I didn't know about contacted me. I knew my grandparents had lived in Charlotte and Gastonia before moving to Fitzgerald, and that my great-grandfather had started and owned a cotton mill in Maysworth, now Cramerton. My father was born there in a house called Maymont. Otherwise, nothing was known to my sisters and me. Daddy Jack never talked about his North Carolina family except once when he mentioned his mean, redheaded stepmother. His own mother, Elizabeth, had died in England when he was seven or so. His father came to America to work in mills and remarried.

Daddy Jack was grown, married, and a father when some terrible rift occurred. He and his father never spoke again, and I never will know what happened.

The distant cousins who read my name in the paper sent me sheafs of information, names of people who would have been my family. Drucilla, Giles, George, Frances, Joseph, Sarah America. In photos, they're all looking out from a Victorian porch. Farther back, Ransom Gray, Narcissa Alexander—thrilling names. Out in her garden, Sarah America stands, stalwart and with a don't-mess-with-me look. For the first time, I saw my great-grandfather's image on his passport application. His passport lists his profession as "cotton mill architect."

I drove down with my sisters, and we saw the big shingled Mayes house now on the historic register in Charlotte, great-grandmother Sarah America Gray Smith's charming, modest cottage in Gastonia, and the big Loray mill her brother founded—the largest cotton mill in the world at that time. This was astonishing. We knew nothing of these people who once had a big world, and in the place I had chosen to live without knowing anything about them. And I carried two of the names: Frances, my father's mother, and Elizabeth, the mother of my grandfather. Coincidence that I came to North Carolina? Some genetic pull toward a family home? Driving around Cramerton, we saw handsome buildings with Mayes Manufacturing over doors, a Mayes school building, and finally a black wrought-iron arch that spelled out *Maymont*. The house was gone.

In the post-Chatwood life, we will have soaring, many-paned windows. My study will be big enough to hold our library, once the seven wall-mounted televisions are removed and bookcases are built. I can have two desks, what luxury, one for spreading out chapters and one for the computer. Best of all, the attic is vaulted and ribbed and there's an oculus. I love the shape of an oculus, as though the building was placed for the light to cross a marker at each solstice.

As I write, we are waiting to sign papers that bind us to another leaving, another homecoming. My house now has a name—Maymont.

Memento Vivere
(Remember to Live)

⚯

In the fall of 2020, when we lived at Three Little Pigs, I went to Italy for two months. In those pre-vaccine days, Americans were banned. Because we have Bramasole, we were allowed under Italian rules to "return to domicile." We have an olive oil business and needed to get back in time for harvest. After brain-probing Covid tests, we took the flying risk while wearing the crucial N95 masks for the seventeen-hour trip (excruciating). The Raleigh-Durham and Philadelphia airports were a breeze, the corridors eerily empty, most businesses closed. On board, everything looked immaculate but I wiped down the earphones, tray, and armrests. Only two others were seated in first class, where we'd cashed in long-banked miles to sit.

Rome FCO was blessedly empty. We were out of there in ten minutes. No one inspected our carefully prepared documents, just waved us through with a *benvenuti*. Francesco, a licensed driver, met us at a designated place. He'd fitted his car with a plastic divide. He turned up the radio and drove the familiar 110 miles an hour home to Cortona, where we quarantined strictly for two weeks.

Will, our grandson, was already here, taking online courses from NYU Shanghai and awaiting his Covid-delayed visa so he could be off to his first year. Online classes would be easier in this time zone. After the botched senior year and drive-by graduation, he was bursting to get out of the four walls of his room. What a boon to spend time with him, even though he slept late, having had Mandarin class at three in the morning. We reveled in our privacy, our books, garden, and slow evenings by the fire. Groceries and wine were delivered. Cooking lavishly for Will, we ate too much lasagne and gelato. Friends left flowers and bread and eggs at the gate.

Italy is a prime travel destination, but for me it always has been the place for a solitary reset. The intimacy of life, the human scale of contact, yes, I've written books about that. Even in a pandemic, the place itself offers balm. Opening my third-floor windows to the wide valley view, finding the book I left, still open to the page where I stopped reading, picking the last of the Sally Holmes and Pierre de Ronsard roses, laying the table, even checking the thresholds for scorpions. With all the return rituals performed, I resumed a life I might never have left.

During quarantine we were consumed—shifting ladders, spreading golden nets under the trees, filling the baskets strapped around our waists with taut green and plumper dark olives. Nature compensated for the lousy year by bestowing a string of halcyon days under a pure blue dome and plenty of Tuscan sun. Picking olives is the best work I know. Will had been here for harvest only once, when he was eight, and he totally got it—the pause for sweet lunches, leaning back against hillsides fresh with unfurling fall ferns and yellow crocuses, the satisfaction of filling a crate with the fruit and picking out the twigs so they don't add tannin to the oil.

No lasagna and red wine with other workers, no celebratory gatherings with neighbors to compare the new oils, no banter in town over whose *resa,* "yield," is best. Although we missed this fun, when we looked up at the Medici fortress and the colossal Etruscan wall over our land, we felt connected with the ancient ritual everyone on this hillside has participated in for centuries uncounted. What joy in this year, when we've all been buffeted and scared and deprived, those of us lucky enough to be only that.

As *la quarantena* ended, I planned a quick work trip to Puglia to complete a writing project, a weekend in Venice, then day trips to see friends in Pienza and Lucignano. After months of seclusion in the United States, freedom dangled within reach! Tuscany was "yellow," meaning some freedoms were permitted.

We had a week. A two-day trip to Florence, a lunch with friends, a meeting in the piazza for coffee. Then the uptick of Covid cases began. Our town was moved to "orange" status, later to "red." Even though there were no cases within the walls, there were some in the surrounding countryside and more in nearby Arezzo. Americans would have been shocked at what real lockdown meant because we never had anything close in the United States. Fill out an online form to go to the grocery store and risk a fine if you stray from your named destination. Temperature checks everywhere. No nonsense about masks: You wear them, even alone outside. Shops, closed. Bars, restaurants, closed or curtailed. Leave home only for exercise walks near your house. No guests. You can't take a drive out of your town. Curfew, of course.

As the poet W. H. Auden wrote, *Our dream of safety has to disappear* . . . Travel plans were squashed flat. We kept busy. Cleaning the garden for winter, planting bulbs, moving the lemon pots into their limonaia (a glass-fronted house for wintering lemons), where they will perfume the glass-fronted room in the months we're gone. Only our neighbors will visit now and then to pluck a few. I harvested a huge basketful and left bags at the gates of friends, preserving the rest in jars with salt and lemon juice.

When I don't know what to do with myself, I plunge into cooking. I ordered a blast of Middle Eastern, Indian, and Turkish spices, various chiles, and other locally unavailable items. Ed and I launched into experimental recipes from *Falastin* and Ottolenghi, which we interspersed with down-home ragù and vegetable pastas. Will loved everything. We made turkey roulade stuffed with veal and pistachios, apple cakes, sage and orange shortbread, ricotta wine cake. I walked it off—well, partly—on Roman roads, listening to audio books—*A Farewell to Arms* and *The End of the Affair*, marvelous, and then *A Dance to the Music of Time* until the characters hopelessly blurred and blended, and I switched to Chopin. Our oil was pressed. Will's visa came through, and we shipped him off to an unknown world to face a severe quarantine but then a marvelous, normal college year due to China's zero-tolerance policies around Covid exposure. His sudden absence felt like a presence. We had no idea when we could see him again. (If I had known it would be a year, I would have been desolate.)

The garden buttoned up. My sweaters sealed in plastic bags. Even my study looked charmingly in order. The weeks danced by to their own music of time, and it was suddenly mid-December. We want to stay; we always want to stay in the deep psychological comfort of this house. A few places I've lived seem to contain a distinct character so that the house is set aside from its inhabitants, existing on its own terms. We love the house's memories—here was an animal manger, under the wine room floor lies a layer of seventeenth-century bricks, beneath the painted walls we know there are remains of landscape frescoes and stenciled arbors, and broad blue and white stripes.

And still there are mysteries—a stone that turned up when a floor was replaced. Carved on its smooth side the Christian IHS. Was that room once a chapel? A bedroom sometimes has whiffs of floral fragrance that caused a priest friend to speculate that a saint's bones are interred in the walls. Far-fetched, but we have no other explanation. Nor can we explain why we have more vivid dreams here than elsewhere, so involving that when I wake up, I don't know where I am. Daylight on objects must orient me again. "Deep into feng shui," a California friend remarked.

We called Francesco to schedule a ride back to Rome for our flight back to the States.

Rome. Rhymes with *home*. My city; Ed's, too. When he first came to Rome, he stepped off the airport bus and said, "I'm home." This I thought unique until several other people told me similar stories.

I knew there would be no tourists. I knew the city was partially shuttered. Ed remarks, "Looks like the day after the

Rapture." Passing the two churches where the Caravaggio paintings live, I imagine seeing them without crowds of viewers elbowing forward. A drizzle begins. We ask Francesco to drop us at 115 on the Corso. He puts our bags on the sidewalk, wishes us *buone feste,* and speeds off, just as we discover we'd given him the wrong street number. Via del Corso, the busiest shopping area in Rome, looks shockingly empty. A few, masked and heads down, walk in the street instead of on the sidewalk. One of those umbrella sellers, who magically appear when three drops have fallen, steps from a doorway. As we lunge the few hundred feet toward the hotel, our roll-on bags clatter on the cobbles, and rain runs in shiny rivulets between the stones, off the tiny umbrellas, and down our backs. For the first time ever in Rome, I catch a whiff of salty sea air. Heavy and humid, along with the pungent char drifting from a lone chestnut-roasting stand on a corner. Overhead the streets strung with lights are lit for *Natale* festivities that are not to happen. I feel a wave of elation. Rome. The city I love best. Beating heart of the Western world.

Part of the pleasure of travel involves projecting a life onto where I am: Ostuni or Oaxaca or Trento or Toronto. Wandering a new town, I pick a neighborhood of stacked sugar-cube houses on a courtyard, an apartment where the canal reflections play on the frescoed ceiling, a whitewashed cottage in a mess of violets and wild irises, or a glass studio eighty floors up, where today is tomorrow. I'd live there, I say. But beyond such easy fantasizing, there's another privately held place in the imagination, a locus of desire, of recurrent dreams, a parallel life. Friends have wistfully described such feelings for Paris, Barcelona, Istanbul, San Francisco,

Hong Kong—where something in the air of the place corre-
sponds to an inner equilibrium. *This is where I am who I am.*
That neverland, primordial-level home where you connect
like prongs in a socket—but where you never, ever in this
lifetime will live.

Of all cities, for me that would be Rome. For many years,
I've tacked on a few days before departures from Fiumicino.
Maybe the precipice of a voyage intensifies the city. My
Roman time always feels fraught because of the scramble to
see what's on at the Quirinale, to try new restaurants, meet
friends at wine bars, shop for gifts, track down ten things on
my to-see list. All this amid a chaos of sirens, horns, weaving
motorcycles, undertows of tourists sucking you down the
street, overflowing garbage bins, buses spilling out groups
from all over the world, silly goofs trying to get in the fountains. I even saw a couple having sex in a doorway, his awful
thrusting butt gleaming white in the moonlight.

This time: Rome alone.

No agenda. I walk. All day. At night. Walking the soles off
my shoes. Ed mostly stays occupied in the hotel, trying to
write three final poems for a manuscript. In this slowed, surreal scape, here's the Rome beneath all the violations. Washed
clean, the city shows its beauty unalloyed. I revisit, even
though many are closed, favorites of mine—Bramante's
Tempietto on the Janiculum Hill, the Baroque extravaganza
Palazzo Colonna, Filippo Lippi's *Annunciation* at splendid
Galleria Doria e Pamphilj, the chalk pastels of palazzi on Piazza San Lorenzo in Lucina, kiosks of botanical prints and severe engravings of ruins at Mercato delle Stampe, Gelateria

del Teatro for sublime tastes of lavender, white peach, cherry, or lime and mascarpone. Who can choose?

At Trevi Fountain, just dark, Ed and I are alone. For the first time in decades, I toss a coin. (One of the earliest movies I remember seeing: *Three Coins in the Fountain*.) At Piazza Navona, too, I hear the musical splash of water from the Four Rivers fountain and walk around the lovely ellipse of the ancient stadium, where once upon a time the perimeter was flooded and navel battles reenacted. At Michelangelo's Piazza Campidoglio, grand Marcus Aurelius, atop his prancing horse, gains in majesty as he surveys a vacant piazza. Totally real, Rome feels as conjured as one of Italo Calvino's invisible cities.

The sycamore trees along the Tevere do not blaze into glory. Instead, they dry, curl, drop. Winter comes late to Rome, if at all, and this December the piled leaves still lend the autumnal scent, complementary to the sienna, ocher, amber colors of the palazzi; to the ancient woman with fright-wig red hair wobbling along the sidewalk with a basket of oranges; to the familiar aroma of serious coffee wafting out of a bar, where the barista stands polishing glasses for no customers. The sky is a color a watercolorist might mix, find it too milky pale, and decide to stir in another dollop of cerulean. The impossible sweetness of the air along the Tevere, and Castel Sant'Angelo, that old horror, anchoring the river view. Trajan's Column seems to tilt against rushing clouds. The forum appears doubly ancient, columns white as bleached femurs. Church bells send out circles of silver sound. The sculptural pines, vulgar magenta bougainvillea, surprise of palms.

Because Rome is "yellow," some restaurants are open for lunch outside. Under heat lamps, we get to order both the fried artichokes and the artichokes with tender homemade pasta. We're talking about the pandemic, talking about whether anything of renewed Rome can be carried forth into normal times. Ed remarks, "In Delhi, residents can see the distant mountains for the first time in decades." We remember the time we showed our grandson eighteen fountains in one day. We remember that Keats rode a pony around the Piazza di Spagna in his last weeks. We remember an apartment we rented with a roof garden that looked down on a clothesline with flapping giant underpants. "On the map of memory," I ask, "doesn't Rome occupy a hemisphere?"

The waiter forgets our glasses of wine, apologizes, and brings over a whole bottle. (That's Rome.) We talk about how deserted the Pantheon is, usually a bedlam of activity. With a friend we loved, we saw it like this one winter during a rare snow: We're alone inside the ancient circle. Our friend suddenly lies down on the floor under the oculus. Flakes falling from on high, land, melt on his face. He was smiling, is smiling still, and I think he looks beatific.

VII

WHY STAY?

SHOULD WE HAVE STAYED AT HOME,
AND THOUGHT OF HERE?
—*Elizabeth Bishop, "Questions of Travel"*

I WANTED TO BE A WRITER. I WANTED TO SAY
SOMETHING ABOUT HOME.
—*Ernest Gaines*

ANNALS OF STONE

Valter, our architect, sketched his plan for the back of the house—a balcony added, a terrace, a broad walkway to a pool around the corner on a flat stretch that used to be our vegetable garden. "Not a 'swimming pool,'" he sneered, "an ornamental seventeenth-century garden pool." I saw alarming visions of cavorting nymphs, urns, fountains. Unlike the meticulous, yard-wide plans rolling out of the vast printers most architects use, this project takes shape on a brown grocery bag. "Do you have a pencil?" Valter will ask, and I then know a vision is taking form. He scratches out what he's drawn and starts over on the other side of the bag.

"Why should we do this?" I asked. We'd called him to consult about a pool.

"Because you can." He gestured across the hillside as if, *whoosh*, the transformation were about to appear.

Since we sold our mountain house outside Cortona, we've missed having a pool. What's a smoldering Tuscan summer without a way to cool off? A pool is a permission broadly granted under otherwise strict architectural controls, no matter if many people put in lurid turquoise gems that can be seen from outer space. No regulation that it's best to blend a pool into green-gray, blue, slate colors of the olive groves and hill-sides.

As we went over the drawings, we hardly noticed the proposed wall running from behind the house to the end of the pool, or other walls sketched here and there. The formal plan was approved by the strict town review over *belli arti* houses. Work began. No nymphs, please, maybe just a melodious cascade of water from the wall abutting the pool. Exciting new outdoor living spaces overlooking the valley and hills. The hole made by the excavation for the technical house, another equipment structure, and a bathroom attached to the house yielded two mountains of stone. I was stunned that just under the surface of our green hillside lay monumental amounts of refrigerator-size boulders, and tons of others the sizes of watermelons and car tires.

Daunting, we began to realize. The inside work we got into was not insignificant. It involved removing bricks between a second- and a third-floor bedroom. How disorienting to look up through beams to the floor above. I had not expected the replacement of plaster but Quinto poked the wall in several spots, showing us where the wall and plaster no longer adhered. How dusty can a house get? Oh, and updating electrical systems, replacing the *cotto* floors in four rooms, adding two bathrooms. The new bathrooms are walled off within existing rooms. Strict as the laws are for every little centimeter outside, no one seems to care how you botch up the inside. We removed an inside back staircase that took up space in already small rooms. I loved the narrow stone stairs but when my grandson was six, he fell from one floor to the next and it was only when he got into universities that I stopped fearing hidden brain damage. After that, every time I looked at the stairs, I remembered the piercing cry. Floors in two rooms had cracked bricks and had to be replaced, which meant replacing the ceiling of the second-floor room.

Our last, I swear, restoration. Ever. This house gets an update and lift now or never. When renovating an old house, one thing leads to the next. That next doubles and squares and soon you're dreaming you're on a trapeze with no bars to catch hold of as you let go and fly through the air. Soon you're complaining that every morning you go out on the balcony and toss a bucket of money to the four winds. And there's this: I love the process.

While Quinto and Gabriele labored inside, four other *muratori*, stonemasons, began that wall we'd hardly noted. Giovanni, Elio, Fabio, and Leo worked, like their predecessors down the thousands of years, with a mallet and a chisel. When "dressed," each stone fits the others like a puzzle piece, every one skillfully placed so that seams are underlined with solid rock. Contiguous cracks would undermine the strength of the wall. Giovanni and Fabio hoist a stone onto a larger flat stone and begin chipping, shaping, eyeing, fitting. Inheritors of an ancient tradition, they're proud. They never seem to weary like Sisyphus, but to arrive at 7:30, break only for a lunch hour, and then clink away until five. They're joking with the other workers, keep up a constant chat, and sometimes sing. Below, Elio and Leo are building other lower walls.

Quinto and Gabriele, also highly skilled masons, break from the inside work to craft stone staircases, brick paths, a balcony.

Back in the USA, I would consider these projects huge but, mysteriously, when I hear fantasy ideas here—make a niche here, build a retaining wall across the flower bed on the steep slope, an arch would be nice—I find myself agreeing and adding on other fantasies—wouldn't two stone banquettes look great along the wall and between them, a stone sink . . . I'm seeing the lavender cushions, pillows with pops of color, guests holding out glasses for a refill. A trunk-size stone caught my eye. Sculptural, it asked to be transformed. Giovanni hollowed out a bowl and a narrow channel for overflow. Now lying in the middle of a rose bed: a Tuscan birdbath. In dreams, statues are hauled from the sea bottom and set up among the roses above the wall. Stone dreams.

My life in the United States involves no stone. For more than thirty years in Tuscany, I have been constantly engaged with some stony project. A fountain. Olive terrace walls that fell. A table made with a rough stone I found on the land, drain covers, an outdoor dining room table, roof supports, steps, benches, raised flower beds, driveway, edging, cistern repair . . . When we first bought Bramasole, Polish workers rebuilt the twelve-foot-tall tumbledown garden terrace wall. Also proud, they inscribed "Polonia" into the base. That wall stupefied us; it seemed a colossal effort. Compared with the current work, that was nothing.

"*Tutto a mano,*" all by hand, says the architect. No power tools were used in the making of this wall. You can read, talk, cook to the rhythmic sounds of stone shaping, but when shrill drilling into concrete enters my head it's as if I'm in the dentist's chair with a gaping cavity that can't be filled.

Every day, before dark, we walk out to see the progress. Eleven months after the wall started, we have endless feet to go.

One mountain of stone has been used.

"Great Wall of China," Ed says.

"How long is the Great Wall of China?"

He takes out his phone and asks. The chirpy robotic voice answers: 13,171 miles.

"Well, this is just a blip."

"Doesn't feel like one. Our shorter one is forty-seven meters. The big wall is out of sight, out of mind."

"Isn't a football field three hundred yards? What's the wall?"

"I hesitate to tell you."

"Why?"

"You're going to melt down. Okay, it's sixty-four meters long."

"So, what's a city block?"

Again, he consults the Delphic oracle. "Forty-seven yards," she says.

"That's perspective. Think of each rock fitted. No wonder it's taking so long." All told: 111 meters.

"Inspiring," Ed says.

"Expensive."

"Beautiful."

When we entered the third round of restoration and additions to Bramasole a year ago, we learned the value of the word *volume*. If you have any shed or shrine or *limonaia*, you may be able to take the volume, the square meters, and build something else, if you destroy said volume. In this *belli arti* zone, without volume you cannot add so much as a bread oven or a place to store the lawn mower. And no, you cannot add a back door or move a window.

We had two bathrooms that were added behind the house, probably in the 1930s, and were now considered *brutto* appendages to the structure. The more primitive of the two consisted only of one toilet, a bucket flush. We'd used the tiny room as a closet after removing the relic. Permission easily granted to rip them off. An old outbuilding for a now-defunct oil tank gave us a few square meters, and a lean-to potting shed donated its space. We were free to construct one new, larger second-floor bathroom opening onto a terrace, and with another terrace on top, which we could enter from the third floor.

"Remember the roof of Fonte?" We are sitting on those stone banquettes I dreamed up and had built along the wall. What a good idea. The old brick tops warm in the sun. This is going to be a prime reading spot. Fonte della Foglia, Font of Leaves, is a stone house we restored in the mountains above Cortona. Bought as an investment, the house cast a spell. After we completed a historic restoration top to bottom, we were unwilling to sell. Some places have *anima*, soul; Fonte was alive with *anima*. After twelve years of juggling two houses in the same town, even we had to admit folly. A lovely English family bought it and I hope live happily ever after.

"We drove all over Tuscany finding those stones." The tumbled house was built by the followers of Saint Francis. Although part of the roof was missing and part was on the ground, enough remained that it deserved restoration. Mossy round, flat stones, centuries old. How could we not?

"How do you feel about building one hundred and eleven meters of stone walls—plus all the steps and borders and low barrier walls that just don't count?"

"Good," Ed answered. "They'll be here when we're dust in the wind, when everyone we know is, too, when our grandson's grandchildren are sunning their booties out by that seventeenth-century ornamental pool."

Excellent answer. I walk along the wall trailing my hand along the smooth and rough and craggy stones. I'm remembering William Butler Yeats's passion for his abandoned tower castle, Thoor Ballylee, and how he longed for a "house of continuance." In my early twenties, when I first crossed the Atlantic and landed in Shannon, I rented a car and set out to see this legendary tower Yeats finally completed and lived in, even though the ground floor flooded constantly in the spring. I was lost and asked a man on a bicycle for directions. "First tower on the right," he said.

Another place with *anima*. A stone on the wall of Yeats's folly reads:

I the poet William Yeats,
With old mill boards and
sea-green slates,
And smithy work from
the Gort forge,
Restored this tower
for my wife George.
And may these characters
remain
When all is ruin once again.

What endures, what fades? I restored this tower, the inscription asserts. Then comes the old realization: *sic transit gloria mundi*.

One May, we rented a noble and funky villa in Puglia with friends. Above the entrance a marble plaque greeted us, as it has countless others. In faint Latin, we made out kind of a welcome mat message from Josephus Martinelli. The words, carved in 1792, were well beyond anyone's high school Latin, but we made out "friends congregate," "soul," "diversion," "hilarity," "genius," and "quiet." At the end, three words: *otium* and *breve negotiosum*. *Otium* is a big concept in Greece and Italy, going all the way back to the ancients. Leisure, contemplation, the good life. *Breve negotiosum* means activity, business—but keep it brief. Josephus apparently expected his hilarious guests to have fully engaged lives—creative, busy times at his blissful country villa, not just lying around sipping vino.

How many hundreds of plaques have I seen on Italian buildings? Memorial, commemorative, historical, poetic. Moss and lichen and weather have obscured meanings. I only can stare and wonder. What I know is that they're all carved on stone. The history of the country is inseparable from stone, and when words are worked into hard surfaces, they get close to immortality, too.

I begin to think we need to leave a message on our wall. Above the center of the pool, where water will spill from a stone chute.

At the August antiques market in Arezzo, I wandered among the stalls, looking for something; I didn't know what until I saw it: a yard-long piece of carved marble, perhaps originally designed to go over a fireplace. Under a scalloped decorative curve was a flat blank space the length of the piece. A perfect place for my note to us, our family, and friends, to those reading it when we are long checked out of five-star Hotel Earth.

Ed said, "Are you sure about this?" He was lifting the plaque. "It weighs—"

"About one hundred pounds," the seller interrupted. He lowered the price by twenty euros.

Ed has exited the market before with table or painting or chair held over his head, joggling through the crowds. The seller wrapped the marble in a blanket and helped hoist it onto Ed's shoulder. I followed, carrying our other purchases.

In Castiglione Fiorentino on the way home, we stopped at the *marmista*, marble worker. Stefano already has been involved with our project. He cut the Carrara tiles for three bathrooms. He is cleaning two old marble sinks that Ed also hauled out of the Arezzo market a few months ago. Why buy expensive ceramic basins when you can find sculptural marble *lavandini* where nuns splashed water on their faces? Stefano's lofty workshop is full of funeral monuments, fine dust, elaborate bathtubs, and slabs of many colors. Of course, he can carve a line on our prize.

What to say?

Weeks go by.

"What will remain of us is love." Philip Larkin's "An Arundel Tomb." Although I would like to, I'm not sure I believe that.

Yeats's gravestone strikes a chilling note:

"Cast a cold Eye on Life, on Death. Horseman, pass by."

I search through Ed's poems, but every evocative line has too many characters for the space.

"Walk on air against your better judgement." Seamus Heaney's "The Gravel Walks." Good. To consider.

Memento vivere became a watchword during the worst of the Covid plague.

I come across a Latin inscription on a medieval sundial.

Ex hoc momento pendet Aeternitas.

"From this moment eternity hinges." Is this what to leave behind for my lovely six-year-old jumping into the water a hundred years from now? Maybe. Or shall I go back to *Memento vivere*, Remember to live?

"I LEFT A BASKET
OF FIGS BY YOUR GATE"

—🗝—

BUSINESS CARDS, EURO COINS, AN ACTION FIGURE, BOTTLES
of wine from Greece, a packet of dill seeds from Finland, a
photo of a baby grinning, dog roses, notes, chocolates from
Poland, dandelions, votive candles, rocks, a hand-embroidered
tablecloth from Romania, a leather bracelet, long letters, wild
fennel fronds, a rose cutting from a Hungarian grandmother's
garden, Christmas ornaments—I find these gifts in the *Madonnina*, shrine to the Madonna, at the entrance to Bramasole.

Years ago, there were only flowers, left by the old man
who walked the mazy roads and stopped to meditate for a few
minutes every day. One summer, he was gone, and by then
my books had been published and translated, and a film had
been made. The house became a magnet.

When walkers, buses, vans, bicycles, and cars began to arrive, I had to wonder what pulled them here. One note
claimed, "We are Bramasolists." A neighbor said we had
more visitors than Santa Margherita, the revered thirteenth-
century saint who lies in a glass coffin in the church of her
name. Another said, "What does it feel like to live in a tourist
attraction?" (At least she didn't say "trap.")

When mementos began to accumulate in our shrine, I

thought of what anthropologists call "threshold gifts," those that mark change. That may be passage from one state of mind, a way out, or a transition from one place to another. A child is born, a marriage takes place, a degree conferred—or you go on a quest. Moments of change inspire gifts. You might think constant visitors would be annoying, but instead, those who come and leave these tokens symbolize something that magnifies why I've stayed in Tuscany for more than thirty years.

I WAS NOT EXPECTING to be the quasi-Italian I became. Even now, my family keeps expecting me to pack up and come back. But I'm staying. If anything, Ed is more rooted than I. "I'm happy," he says often. "I'm happy to see this view every day." "I'm happy because the days are unpredictable." We've lived in Tuscany—and in airline seats—longer than anywhere else.

What the somewhat innocent abroad that I was would learn: Living in a beautiful landscape changes you. When simple, everyday life feels like a gift, you respond in surprising ways.

The gift exchange runs rampant through my days. Not just notes and rose cuttings from strangers, which I love, but the constant generosity and thoughtfulness among those who always live here.

A bag of fresh ricotta hanging on the gate, a bottle of new wine, a basket of Claudio's eggs, a bucket full of zinnias, jars of tomatoes. "I thought of you when I saw these notepads." Figs, melons, duck ragù. "Try my new oil." More wine, always wine. The workers on our building project go home to their villages in the south and return with marvelous loaves of bread for us. (They scorn the unsalted Tuscan bread.) They grill at lunch and spread the table with sausages, steak, ribs, and veal chops. They organize dinners at restaurants for us and the whole crew. I'm the only woman with twenty guys.

In town, "Oh, Roberto has paid for your coffee." Purchases of sweaters, jackets, stationery, jewelry, usually include a *sconto*, a nice discount. In your bag of vegetables, you'll find a gift—parsley, basil, a stalk of celery and a carrot, *odori*, the basis of *soffritto*, the little flavors to sauté for pasta sauces.

These daily gifts, freely given with no expectation of return, go the distance in creating a close sense of community. The expats who move here pick up on the local customs quickly after arrival. Soon they're receiving the bag of persimmons and the slab of pecorino and the single big porcino mushroom, presented with a big grin. Then the expats are arriving at dinners with jars of apricot preserves, *pensieri*, little thoughts, from their travels—scarves, soaps, candles, books. It's catching. Electric. You pay it forward. The giving—it's a transformative proposition because when you give, something opens inside you, too. For my part, these gifts give me a chance to feel at home in the world.

I signed stacks of papers in the notary office that day long ago when the house became mine, never thinking beyond a few summers into the future. If the notary had said, "Three decades from now, you'll still own this house," I would have looked at her with wonder or alarm. I thought I would return mainly to write, travel with Ed, and to restore the house and garden. My university job was demanding. My real life was elsewhere. This new life seemed almost extraterrestrial. Bra-masole was to be a summer haven, a background to expanses of time for friends, books, love, and art.

Why stay? Seasons and years passed and still I never think of leaving. I love my third-floor study. Two desks, and books, books, books. My neighbors are family. Chiara was a teenager when we came; her six-year-old daughter now brings me bas-kets of foraged leaves, chestnuts, grasses, and sticks. Winter falls hard; the twilight starts at four, and the table is set for long dinners. Music plays in the kitchen and boiling pasta water steams the windows. We've built grape pergolas out where the view is widest. Will has a desk full of Italian home-work sheets, models of Vespas and sailboats in the drawers. My daughter keeps a pink bathrobe and slippers in an *arma-dio*. But all that isn't unique to this place.

Let's just sit out on the wall with a glass of wine, joking and watching the blue moon rise out of the hills. Let's think about this. Why stay?

From the first day, I should have realized: The house is *not* background. It lives a life on this hillside that affirms the sun-rise, that placemarks the Etruscan wall, anchors the olive ter-races, and oversees views of valleys and hills. We, on the other hand, are passing through.

Certainly, we've left markers—thank you very much: We have secured the structure at huge expense. This charmed little villa will stand ages hence. Was it waiting all along for the person who would care the most? The place made my books, and my books made the place. Or—did the house write back to its author? A "house of continuance," Yeats wanted. This is one.

Forgive the personification, easy to fall into when a house simmers with life. Of course, the house does not write back. I'll just say I stay because gifts accumulate. Gifts, those of the natural life of this hillside. And of others. Through letters and book signings and just meeting people in the piazza, my life expanded. I connected with people from New Haven to New Delhi. I became a confidant to strangers who often felt like friends I would have if I lived where they live. One wrote, "I knew, walking down that aisle, that I didn't love him enough." I read "I'm giving up law to study Italian cooking." Many were concerned over my lack of traditional faith, sending religious books. Others left woven dishcloths, an embroidered tablecloth, a painting of the house.

All this complements what was already the way of living I fell into, easy as a canoe nudging into the stream.

From where did this constant exchange arise? Here, I'll make a leap. From the arts. According to UNESCO, Italy owns 60 percent of the world's most important art. A confounding fact, given that Italy is close to the size of Arizona. Some say half of that art is in Florence. But don't forget the Fra Angelico *Annunciation* in Cortona, the Signorelli Judgment Day fresco cycle in Orvieto, and the thousands of other works in small places all over Italy. In Troia, residents have looked up at the duomo's magnificent lacy stone rose window every day since 1039. In Monterchi, no one needs reminding that the majestic *Madonna del Parto* resides there because it was the home of Piero della Francesca's mother. The Madonna, shown pregnant, still gives local women a place to pray, a natural tie to the sublime. I could go on for infinite pages. Art, a shower of gifts.

I first came to Italy for the art. I wanted to see all the paintings and sculptures I'd seen on slides in art history classes. I was not wrong. From the Uffizi in Florence to the smallest country chapels, I've thrived on the surprises of art. Living where art is everywhere and is taken as part of normal life pushes me to extrapolate on my foray into the joys and meaning of living in a gift culture. What if the fabulous generosity of Italian life evolves from the heritage of art? I experience the plethora of art as gifts. Grazie Bronzino, Pontormo, Lippi, Masaccio, *grazie mille*. Their immense talents were gifts to them, and the art they created are gifts showered onto us.

I used to teach my graduate creative writing students a book called *The Gift: Imagination and the Erotic Life of Property* by Lewis Hyde. We started the semester with this book because Hyde wrote about the meanings of gifts, how gifts work in art, in tribal cultures, and in folklore. Art is catching. There's a simpatico circulation, and who knows where the concentric rings of an artistic gift end? Hyde says: ". . . a circulation of gifts nourishes those parts of our spirit that are not entirely personal, parts that derive from nature, the group, the race, or the gods."

What I value most in his book are the ideas I thought crucial to anyone setting out to be a writer, composer, dancer, painter, sculptor. The desire to make art is itself a gift you are given. He quotes D. H. Lawrence's acknowledgment of this: "Not I, not I, but the wind that blows through me." To produce a book or cello concerto, aria, or portrait becomes a de facto gift to others, not only the gift of pleasures and enlightenment received but also the inspiration for other art.

Giving any gift, he teaches, "creates that empty place into

which new energy may flow." The recipient is awarded, and the one who gives is spiritually replenished. This works at the level of Leonardo da Vinci and the one who leaves a basket of figs. At age eleven, wandering the shelves of the Carnegie Library in Fitzgerald, I thought, *This is the best thing you can be—a writer.* Even a novice who feels the urge toward creativity already imagines the gift.

I have to think that the girls' group from Warsaw who began singing their national anthem at the gate, and the entwined couple roaring up on the Moto Guzzi, and the artist sketching by the road are all pondering change, choice, taking a small chance, or a radical leap toward home. *Where do you eat in Verona? How do you write a novel? Where do you start?* As Dante's *The Divine Comedy* begins, you reach impenetrable woods. *Where do you go?*

A Wednesday morning alone in the Galleria Borghese, and thinking for the first time of each sculpture and painting as a gift, today, just for me. How intimate the works become. Ghirlandaio's *Leda,* his *Lucretia.* The often-reproduced Roman boy pulling a thorn from his foot. How can you refrain from running your hand over the pellucid marble *Sleeping Hermaphroditus?*

Perugino. Raffaello. Seemingly everyone who lifted a brush. I walk out into the dusty park like one in love. And how common this experience. To be soaked and stirred and revived. Whatever gods, or powers, or forces, the blessings of art were poured over Italy. We're the lucky recipients. What will we, who are immersed in this culture, who live as if at home, give back?

Today, coffee from Torino. Books. A manuscript sent for

comment. Emails—*"I'm starting my own catering business." "I was the TA in a Shakespeare class you took. Can I visit?"* The motif of all: how to change; how to choose, yes, but bottom line: the spontaneous sharing. *I made these potholders in rehab. I went because . . .*

Only connect, E. M. Forster wrote. *Make good choices,* I whisper.

Envoi:
Architect

From the street, the house I built resembles a tall, tawny stone wall. The roof appears flat but slopes slightly downward for rain to glide toward the garden. Is this a house I built? Along the gutters, the iron mouths of six dolphins spill water into a pebble channel, which flows along the front of the house, curves around to the rear, and under a curved bridge leading to the back entrance. I hear the sluice, jingle, and fall—water over rocks. Who's home? The glass doors could slide apart for me but instead I turn toward the walled garden—all green, no flowers—where I hid a small woven osier bower with one chair and a glass bell hanging from the arch. Although I designed the house, I do not go inside. What is this house's name?

When such images linger in the morning, I imagine who will live there, shut off from the street, doors opening to green solitude and the wide feeling of belonging.

Who does not love a tower? A swirl of sand rises off the beach and the house I build is circular and rising, with nautilus-chambered rooms facing the sea. I've indulged in dark sapphire silk-velvet sofas, though some of the furniture is made of books. The instant happiness of Vivaldi cascades down the staircase, the unfrozen music part of the architecture.

One night, there is only a kitchen and I build in a large chopping board because to chop is the main task in any kitchen where savory aromas rise from copper pots. Why haul out flimsy acrylic boards that stain and must be scrubbed with salt and lemon? The kitchen's metal windows crank out for the cat to exit. Two moon-shaped lights suspend over marble counters the color of malachite. I trace tiny fossils with my nail. The exceptionally sharp knife I bought in Florence gleams on the counter. Etched on the blade, what's that, the word *plumeria*. This must be a dream says the dream.

I GO BACK TO the yellow house. Mine now, mine to give to my mother. All fretwork comes down to be stripped, painted, and reattached. I work on this, sandpaper rough on my hands, the pronged ring she gave me sliding off over and over. The porch will have ferns, palms, and chintz cushions on the wicker. On the back balcony, I see the droopy string and the wooden clothespins to hang my small things to dry. Down, down the dogleg stairs, I assure someone that the dividing wall must come down. I insist. A mirror at the end of the hall glares so hard that I can't see anyone reflected. Only a triangle of russet skirt.

Best nights, when the meaning of a dream is the dream itself. (Put up a wall against the strife of the *agora*.) I cover my face with the music of falling water. Go back to the oldest desires. Be practical. I give my mother the surprise. (Slip away.)

The stone steps are etched with lichen. A glass door cracks open.

I know they're in there, all the ones I love with all the ones I lost. Sprawled on cushions, reading, or gathering in the kitchen around the cakes and wine. They are by now at home in this world, although home is an enigma inside a conundrum, dipped in acid, rinsed in rain, shiny slick as a newborn, a place under the skin, under the moon, a pivot, a bolt-hole, and a floor plan of planet Earth.

ACKNOWLEDGMENTS

PUBLICATION ACKNOWLEDGMENTS

My thanks to the editors who first published some of these chapters (sometimes in other versions) in the following publications:

Afar
Atlanta
Dream of Venice, edited by JoAnn Locktov,
    Bella Figura Publications
A Fork in the Road: Tales of Food, Pleasure and
    Discovery on the Road, edited by
    James Oseland, Lonely Planet
Garden & Gun
The New York Times
Our State
The Oxford American
Shrines: Images of Italian Worship, by Steven Rothfeld
    and Frances Mayes, Doubleday
Southern Living
South Writ Large
Thoughts of Home, edited by Elaine Greene, Hearst Books
Victoria
Walter

PERSONAL
ACKNOWLEDGMENTS

I'm grateful to my editors at Crown: Hilary Teeman and Aubrey Martinson. They are pros and great to work with. Caroline Weishuhn, thanks for graceful help with the manuscript. I've been lucky through several books to work with insightful publicists, Rachel Rokicki and Gwyneth Stansfield. To the jacket designer, Christopher Brand, heartfelt thanks. And thanks to Melissa Esner, Cindy Berman, Barbara Bachman, and the rest of the team at Crown. Special thanks to Crown's brilliant leaders, Annsley Rosner and David Drake.

This book is dedicated to my wonder agent Peter Ginsberg of Curtis Brown Ltd. We've been together since I cold-called so long ago and said "I've written this memoir about restoring a house in Tuscany. Would you take a look?" Again, thank you, Peter, for your humor, tenacity, and insight. I always will remember my longtime editor, Charlie Conrad, and Audrey Wells, screenwriter and director of the movie *Under the Tuscan Sun*. Much gratitude to Steven Barclay and Eliza Fischer at The Steven Barclay Agency for the chance to speak at many fundraisers and other marvelous events. Special love and thanks to John Beerman and Tori Reynolds.

How impossible to thank the many friends I have cherished over the years this book covers. I will raise a glass with you when next we are together. Some are lost but are always with me. *Cin cin* to Lee Smith for long walks and deep talks, to my Hillsborough writers' group—Francesca Talenti, Elisabeth Benfy, Margaret Rich, Nancy Demorest, Samia Serageldin—

and to the raucous, close-reading Traveling Book Club in Cortona. *Tanti saluti* to the inspiring Silvia Baracchi, Ondine Cohane, Debbie and Hans Rosenstein, Steven Rothfeld, Susan Swan, Aurora Patrito, and my Italian brother, Fulvio di Rosa.

Thank you, *amici*, who allowed me to write about your food memories and your houses. Great thanks to Gilda di Vizio, Fabio Pelucchini, and Giorgio Zappini. I have always wanted to write about my friends' unique houses. This book about facets of home gave me the chance to wander rooms and to set down my fascinations: Kate Abbe (now deceased but her house is vivid in memory), Jane Holding, Lee Smith, Fred Stewart, Jimmy Holcomb, Ann Stewart, Steven Burke, Randy Campbell, Michael Malone, Maureen Quilligan, Susie and Rowan Russell, Susan Wyler, Allan Gurganus, Elspeth and Clay Willcoxon, Margaret Henderson, Francesca Talenti, Jean and Azia Cami, Coco and Jim Pante. And to these friends, too, my thanks for their food memories: Sheryl Turping, Susie and Rowan Russell, Coco and Jim Pante, Jean Cami, and Jane Holding.

To Will, whose code name is Tailwind, we'll meet you wherever. To my daughter, Ashley, and her husband, Peter, I cherish every moment with you. Book the tickets! A once-again Bramasole restoration awaits. To Ed, *da cuore*, wherever you are, we're home.

A NOTE ON SOURCES

Most of the quotes I've used are identified in the text. Additionally, on page xxiii, the quote from Carson McCullers is from "Look Homeward, Americans," *Vogue*, December, 1940. On page 6, for information on the Occaneechi tribe, go to ncpedia.org/occaneechi-indians. On page 10, the author of *A Long, Long Way* is Sebastian Barry. The quote on page 26 is from "God's Grandeur" by Gerard Manley Hopkins. On page 123, find more on Eudora Welty in *More Conversations with Eudora Welty* by Peggy Prenshaw. On page 33, the "Twice or thrice" quote is from John Donne's "Air and Angels." On page 151, see more information on the Wanderer at jekyllisland.c/the-water-and-the-blood. On page 60, the William Faulkner quote is from *Requiem for a Nun*. On page 189, see *When Women Ruled the World* by Maureen Quilligan. On page 110, the quote is attributed to Santayana but probably is by Robert Lowell parodying Santayana.

Under the Tuscan Sun was FRANCES MAYES's first book about Italy. Previously, she published six books of poetry and a popular college textbook, *The Discovery of Poetry*. Her Italian memoirs *Bella Tuscany* and *Every Day in Tuscany* followed *Under the Tuscan Sun*, along with *In Tuscany, Bringing Tuscany Home, A Year in the World,* and *The Tuscan Sun Cookbook*. She has also written the travel narratives *See You in the Piazza* and *Always Italy,* the novel *Swan,* and a southern memoir, *Under Magnolia*. Her most recent novel, *Women in Sunlight,* takes place in Italy.

Frances and her poet husband, Edward Mayes, live at Bramasole in Cortona, Tuscany, where it all began, and in Durham, North Carolina.

This book was set in Fournier, a typeface named for Pierre-Simon Fournier (1712–68), the youngest son of a French printing family. He started out engraving woodblocks and large capitals, then moved on to fonts of type. In 1736 he began his own foundry and made several important contributions in the field of type design; he is said to have cut 147 alphabets of his own creation. Fournier is probably best remembered as the designer of St. Augustine Ordinaire, a face that served as the model for the Monotype Corporation's Fournier, which was released in 1925.